Multifaith

Information
Manual

Multifaith Information Manual

© Ontario Multifaith Council on Spiritual and Religious Care, 1995.

Canadian Cataloging in Publication Data

Main entry under title:

Multifaith Information Manual

[3rd ed.]
Includes bibliographical references.
ISBN 1-896377-00-9

1. Religions. 2. Pastoral Counselling. I. Turner,
B. Kali. II. Ontario Multifaith Council on
Spiritual and Religious Care.

BL80.2.M85 1995   291   C95-930730-3

Ontario Multifaith Council on Spiritual and Religious Care
35 McCaul St., Suite 200
Toronto, ON M5T 1V7

Editing: B. Kali Turner
Cover Design & Art: Jeff Combee, Graphic House Associates
Design & Production: Brian D. Minielly
Printed in Canada by: W. D. Keeling Printers Ltd.

Copies of this book are available for a charge from the Multifaith Council and various book dealers. See the listings for this and related items in Appendix B.

Table of Contents

ACKNOWLEDGEMENTS

This is the third edition of a reference guide for spiritual and religious care-givers and resource persons. Like the previous versions, the new **Multifaith Information Manual** reflects the broad spectrum of discipline and practice which are the celebration of spirituality in our diverse communities. It has been enlarged, reformatted and re-written in response to readers' feedback to make it more convenient and useful.

Credits at the end of each section identify the individual or group responsible for the content and approvals for each faith tradition. The traditions presented here reflect the diversity of our clients, and we thank the many people who worked with the editor, Kali Turner, for their hard work and perseverance. It is difficult to take the authentic presentations of so many diverse faith traditions and work them into a standard format. We hope that the flexibility of the manual's design will assist the reader while retaining the unique characteristics of each tradition.

The Ontario Multifaith Council on Spiritual and Religious Care is an advocate for spiritual care and religious rights. It works in support of chaplains and other care-givers. This manual is a celebration of the diversity of the human spirit. We would like to acknowledge the many citizens who find themselves in institutions, vulnerable and facing challenges and crises with courage. In the struggle to make meaning of their circumstances, they draw on the support and understanding of many people, family, friends, volunteers and professional caregivers.

INTRODUCTION

The provision of spiritual and religious care in the Ontario Public Service is supported by the member faith traditions which comprise the Ontario Multifaith Council on Spiritual and Religious Care. These collaborating faith groups are 'partners' with the provincial government through programmes in three ministries (Community and Social Services, Health, and Solicitor General & Correctional Services). The concept and realization of this manual have evolved from work begun in 1986. Throughout the evolution of this document, the principle of presenting the authentic voice of each faith tradition has been a constant. It is retained and enhanced in this edition.

As an ever wider network of chaplains became aware of this resource information package, we received numerous requests from across the country and internationally. This growing demand changed the Multifaith Council's practice of some twenty years in resource distribution. These changes include the creation of a new standing committee, the Publishing Trust, to coordinate the development and distribution of multifaith materials. Other items are being prepared to further support multifaith education abd practice. Appendix One lists some of the current materials.

The Multifaith Council is redefining the role of the chaplain, creating new responses to the need for educational materials and current resources, and inventing new approaches to professional development for chaplains. This is a creative response to the growing diversity of the province's population, the move to community-based services, as well as the stresses and pressures being experienced by faith groups as well as all publicly funded services.

Through it all the Multifaith Council has tried to keep paramount its united concern for the individual's spirit and the diversity of their respective faith traditions. That spirit and intent is reflected in these pages.

Brian Minielly
Chair, OMC Publishing Trust Committee
Bahá'í Representative

TO THE READER:

While this manual has been created to be as unified and systematic as possible, certain discrepancies may still exist in the wording and format. This is due to the diversity of the manual's content.

The groups themselves often requested certain phrasing, to which we tried to acquiesce. Thus, the chapters retain the style and essence of their original writers.

BAHÁ'Í FAITH

FOUNDER

Baha'u'llah (meaning "The glory of God"), (1817 - 1892).

NATURE OF RELIGION

Monotheistic

SCRIPTURES

Works by the Bab (forerunner), Baha'u'llah, and his son 'Abdu'l-Baha. The works of Shoghi Effendi (grandson of 'Abdu'l-Baha) are considered authoritative, but not sacred.

BASIC BELIEFS

- The oneness of God, the oneness of religion, and the oneness of humanity.
- The purpose of religion is to unify humanity.
- All great religions and prophets are divine in origin.
- All great religions represent successive stages of divine revelation throughout human history.
- The eradication of racial and religious prejudice.
- The search for truth as an individual responsibility.
- The harmony of religion and science as complementary aspects of the truth.
- The establishment of an international auxiliary language.
- Basic education for all children.
- Abolition of extreme wealth and poverty.
- Equality of the sexes.

MODE OF WORSHIP

Daily prayer and reading of Baha'i sacred writings is the individual's responsibility. All work performed in the spirit of service is also considered to be worship. Therefore all individuals are enjoined to develop a craft, trade or profession. The 19-day Feast (please refer to the *Baha'i Calendar*) is a time of community prayer, readings, consultation and socializing. Since there is no "church", feasts are often held in private homes, a rented hall or a Baha'i Centre.

STRUCTURE

Local, national and international elected administrative institutions are responsible for guidance, protection, education and legal affairs. Wherever 9 or more Baha'i adults gather in each locality, they elect a local, 9-member Spiritual Assembly. Local and National Assemblies are elected annually. The Universal House of Justice, elected once every 5 years, is located in Haifa, Israel.

DIVISIONS/DENOMINATIONS

None

RITUALS

Daily private prayer and an annual fast, lasting throughout the day from sunrise to sunset during March 2 to March 20.

LAWS

- Marriage requires the consent of both parties and their parents.
- Men and women must observe chastity before marriage, and fidelity within marriage.

- Consumption of alcohol or mind-altering drugs is forbidden, except when prescribed by a physician.

- Involvement in partisan politics is not allowed.

- Backbiting is forbidden.

- Mendicancy and asceticism are forbidden.

MODE OF DRESS/MODESTY REQUIREMENTS

None

DIETARY REQUIREMENTS

None

HOLY DAYS/FESTIVALS

DAYS ON WHICH ONE SHOULD ABSTAIN FROM WORK OR SCHOOL

Ridvan: April 21, April 29, & May 2
The period during which Baha'u'llah declared his mission (Baghdad 1863). Ridvan is also the period during which the elections of the Local and National Spiritual Assemblies take place every year.

Declaration of the Bab: May 23 (Iran, 1844)
The Bab announced the new faith and himself as the Forerunner of the "One Whom God Shall Make Manifest", Baha'u'llah.

Ascension of Baha'u'llah: May 29 Anniversary of Baha'u'llah's death in 1892 in Akka, Palestine, concluding 40 years of captivity and exile.

Martyrdom of the Bab: July 9
Anniversary of the Bab's execution by firing squad in Tabriz, Iran, 1850.

Birth of the Bab ("The Gate"): October 20
The Bab was born in Shiraz, Iran, 1819.

Birth of Baha'u'llah: November 12
Baha'u'llah was born in Tehran, Iran, 1817.

Naw Ruz (New Year): March 21
The first day of the year in the Baha'i calendar.

Days on which one may work

Day of the Covenant: November 26
Celebration of 'Abdu'l-Baha's appointment as the authorized interpreter and the "Centre of the Covenant" to safeguard the unity of the Baha'i community. 'Abdu'l-Baha was the "Servant of the Glory", Baha'u'llah's eldest son.

Ascension of 'Abdu'l-Baha: November 28   Anniversary of his death in Palestine, 1921.
Intercalary Days: February 26 - March 1
These 4 days (5 in leap year) fall between the last 2 months of the Baha'i calendar, and are days of celebration, charitable works, gift-giving and hospitality.
The Baha'i Fast: March 2 - 20
Baha'is over the age of 15 who are in good health abstain from food and drink from sunrise until sunset each day.

Beliefs and Practices Regarding Death
Beliefs

An individual's essence or reality is spiritual, not physical; the body is seen as the throne of the soul, worthy to be treated with honour and respect even though it may be dead. After physical death, the soul continues to progress; it proceeds on to the next stage of existence, closer to God, free of physical limitations.

Practices

The body should be buried, not cremated; preferably without embalming (unless embalming is required by law). It must not be transported more than one hour's journey from the place of death. For a Baha'i over 15 years old, the Prayer for the Dead is to be recited at burial.

Special Religious Rituals which can be Performed only by an Authorized representative of this faith

In cases of marriage, death and funerals, the chaplain is expected to contact the nearest Spiritual Assembly or the National Baha'i Centre at Thornhill.

Sacred writings required

For private worship; Baha'i Prayers

Sacred objects required

None

SYMBOLS

The symbol most frequently used for the Baha'i faith is the 9 - Pointed star.

BAHA'I CALENDAR

This solar calendar begins on March 21 and consists of 19 months of 19 days each, with 4 "intercalary" days. Each local Baha'i community gathers for a "feast" on the first day of each month. At the feast, there is a sharing of devotions, community business, and a time of socializing. Baha'i days begin and end at sunset.

This chapter was contributed by:
The Baha'i National Centre
The Baha'i Community of Canada
Department of Public Affairs
7200 Leslie Street
Thornhill, Ontario
L3T 6L8   (905) 889-8168

BUDDHISM

FOUNDER

Lord Shakyamuni Buddha, 539 B.C.

NATURE OF RELIGION

- Study of the Mind to Attain Liberation from Suffering, Enlightenment and the State of Buddhahood.
- A Profound Paradigm of Psychology, Spiritual Philosophy and Practice to Liberate All Beings from Suffering.
- Personal insight replaces belief in God with the complete study of the Laws of Cause and Effect - Karma.

- Basic Tenet - Reincarnation

- Buddhism is essentially a monastic religion, with novice and full ordination for monks and nuns. However, Lord Buddha also taught spiritual practices for lay people to follow. The emphasis here will be on the practices for lay people.

SCRIPTURES

Basic types of Scriptures:
Hinayana: Tripitaka
Mahyana: Sutra
Varajyana: Lam Rim

BASIC TEACHINGS (BELIEFS)

All paths of Buddhism embrace the following basic teachings of Lord Shakyamuni Buddha, **THE FOUR NOBLE TRUTHS.**

THE FIRST NOBLE TRUTH - DUKKHA

Ordinary existence is a State of Suffering.

The Three Types of Suffering:

1. Physical Suffering: This includes birth, sickness, old age and death.

2. Impermanence: Impermanence pervades all things.

3. Mental Suffering: Mental Suffering consists of conditioned states. It is the worst of all suffering, leading to a negative mind and affecting all aspects of life. Eventually, this negative mind leads to rebirth into one of the three lower realms; one of the hell realms, the hungry ghostrealm or the animal realm. The negative, unvirtuous mind causes the following effects:

   Body: Killing, stealing and sexual exploitation of others.

   Speech: Lying, angry words, slander and meaningless gossip.

   Mind: Ignorance, greed, anger.

THE SECOND NOBLE TRUTH - THE ARISING OF DUKKHA

Cause of Suffering

Suffering is caused by an ignorant state of mind. We have been misinformed by our culture and lack LORD BUDDHA'S teachings; hence, bondage to a false reality.

THE THIRD NOBLE TRUTH - THE CESSATION OF DUKKHA

End of Suffering

Suffering is ended by renouncing the negative mind, developing loving kindness and compassion for all beings, and by cutting out the root of ignorance, which brings about understanding of the true nature of reality. This causes personal liberation from suffering and lasting peace of mind. Such realization creates harmonious relationships between oneself, all beings and the environment.

THE FOURTH NOBLE TRUTH - THE PATH

Embracing the teachings of LORD BUDDHA.

The only method by which one can attain liberation from suffering is to follow the path of Buddhism. This requires mental discipline and the actual practice of LORD BUDDHA'S teachings, which involves many lifetimes of devoted effort and commitment.

The Eight-Fold Noble Path: (for Lay People only)

Wisdom
1.   Right Understanding
2.   Right Intention

Ethical Discipline
3.   Right Speech
4.   Right Action
5.   Right Means of Livelihood

Mental Discipline
6.   Right Effort
7.   Right Mindfulness
8.   Right Concentration

Five Precepts: (For Lay People only)

The five precepts deal with all aspects of life; body, speech and mind. (A person may undertake 1 to 5 of these vows, depending upon one's ability to keep them purely.)

Body
1.   Abstention from killing.
2.   Abstention from stealing.
3.   Abstention from sexual exploitation.

Speech
4.   Abstention from lying.

Mind
5.   Abstention from all drugs and intoxicants which alter the mind.

SPIRITUAL PRACTICE (MODE OF WORSHIP)

Typically, people meet in temples or centres to learn spiritual practices in a group, then follow up with individual practice at home.

STRUCTURE

Ordained Spiritual Community: This involves full ordination for women and men and requires hundreds of precepts. Novice ordination for women and men requires far fewer precepts. The number of precepts in both cases depends upon the school of Buddhism.

Lay Spiritual Community: Lay vows for women and men. These require the five basic precepts.

There are no institutionally organized hierarchical structures. However, qualified practitioners can determine different levels of personal realization. Hence, people with higher levels of realization are teachers of Buddhism and are usually ordained Sangha.

DIVISIONS/DENOMINATIONS

The Three Paths of Buddhism:

The Lesser Vehicle: **HINAYANA:**
Tripitika - Foundation Practices for all Schools of Buddhism.
Theravada: India, Burma, Thailand, Cambodia, Laos and Sri Lanka.

The Greater Vehicle: **MAHAYANA:**
Sutra - Path of the Bodhisattva (includes Foundation practices).
Ch'an: China
Zen: Korea, Japan and Vietnam.

The Diamond Vehicle: **VAJRAYANA:**
Lam Rim - Secret Tantra and Mantra (includes Foundation Practices and Path of the Bodhisattva).
Tibetan Buddhism: India and Tibet.

RITUALS

Buddhist rituals include blessing and giving of Dharma name to baby, providing refuge to Buddha, Dharma and Sangha, conferring lay vows of morality, conferring of Bodhisattva vows and teachings of Buddha Dharma. As well, instruction in various forms of Buddhist meditation and individual Buddhist spiritual counselling is necessary. Buddhists also practice lengthy pre-death counselling and rituals.

Each of Buddhism's many lineages has its own schedule for spiritual celebrations unique to its particular lineage, with one exception. The highest spiritual celebration, WESAK, being Shakyamuni Buddha's Birth, Enlightenment and Paranirvana, is shared by all lineages. This date and a number of others are indicated on the Multifaith calendar.

LAWS

Buddhists adhere to and study the Laws of Cause and Effect (Karma), that all suffering is caused by unvirtuous actions of body, speech and mind, and that all happiness is caused by virtuous actions of body, speech and mind.

MODE OF DRESS/MODESTY REQUIREMENTS

Lay people are to dress in modest attire reflecting the virtuous mind, appropriate to the culture in which they live.

DIETARY REQUIREMENTS

Dietary requirements vary, depending upon the School. In some instances, vegetarianism is expected. Generally speaking, Buddhism recommends people eat foods that are grown in their particular location of the world. As well, people are recommended to eat food that is needed for their unique health requirements, which may not necessarily be vegetarian.

HOLY DAYS/FESTIVALS

The Buddhist calendar is as varied as the different schools and traditions that make up international Buddhism. While some celebrations are common to all Buddhists, many are unique to particular schools.

Significant to all Buddhists everywhere is the life and teachings of LORD SHAKYAMUNI BUDDHA, who is the Buddha for this age, and lived in India, ca. 560-480 B.C.. Events related to LORD BUDDHA may be celebrated at different times in different temples, but the full moon and new moon are commonly recognized as the most important days of celebration.

The list of festivals given in The *Multifaith Calendar* includes four directly associated with the life of LORD BUDDHA (Wesak, Day of Miracles, Dhamma Day and Merit-sharing Day). Two relate to the Sangha or the ordained community, namely, Wassa (Beginning of Rains Retreat) and Pavarana (End of Retreat). The other three are both religious and secular; the Chinese New Year and the Tibetan New Year (February), the (Theravadan) Saka New Year (April), and Founders Day (October), which marks two events of special importance for Canadian Buddhists. These are the formal introduction of Buddhism to Canada in 1905 and the first assembly of Buddhists of Toronto in 1980, which led to the formation of the Buddhist Council of Canada.

Note: Used with permission of the *Multifaith Calendar*, Canadian Ecumenical Action, Vancouver

BASIC TENET AND PRACTICE REGARDING DEATH

BASIC TENET

Buddhism follows the basic tenet that rebirth is an existing reality. Death is regarded as the actual time of movement from one life to another. All rituals at death are aimed at promoting an auspicious human rebirth in the next life, as well as preventing lower forms of rebirth taking place, such as rebirth into one of the hell realms, the hungry ghost realm or the animal realm.

It is imperative that a Buddhist representative be notified well in advance to see that an appropriately ordained Monk or Nun presides over the care of a dying person.

PRACTICE (FOR INSTITUTIONAL STAFF)

Once the person loses consciousness and he or she no longer has the ability to interact with others, his or her physical comfort is no longer an issue. The individual should then be placed on the gurney. This is the time to remove all devices. He or she should remain on this gurney until cremation.

When the individual is pronounced "dead", the body should be gently covered with a cotton sheet, with care taken not to create any disturbance to it. It must not be touched, manipulated or moved around by another person's hand or body. Do not close the eyes, mouth, etcetera. Leave the body just as it is.

Additionally, no talking, crying, or any other noise whatsoever is allowed. This can be done away from the body in another room. At an appropriate time, gently set the gurney in motion and push quietly to the cold storage room, being careful not to bump the gurney on the way. As well, the attendant should be silent, completely refraining from speech along the way.

Place the gurney at the back of the cold storage area, where it will not be subject to movement in any way whatsoever for the following three days or until the ceremony is conducted. The body should remain in cold storage for three days or until the appropriate religious ceremony can be performed by Ordained Sangha. After this ceremony has been performed, the body may be removed from the gurney and prepared for cremation.

SPECIAL RELIGIOUS RITUALS WHICH CAN BE PERFORMED ONLY BY AN AUTHORIZED REPRESENTATIVE OF THIS FAITH

These must be performed by ordained monks or nuns of the Buddhist community.

SACRED WRITINGS REQUIRED

Not Applicable

SACRED OBJECTS REQUIRED

- Shrine Table
- Statue of LORD BUDDHA
- Texts and Scriptures
- Pictures
- Meditation Cushions
- Rosary Beads
- Incense

- Flowers
- Candles
- Fruit
- Table Cloth
- Gongs
- Bells
- Drums

SYMBOLS

These symbols characterize Buddhism:

- The Double Dorje represents the Enlightened Mind.
- The Three Jewels represent refuge in Buddha, Dharma and Sangha.
- The Dharmachkra represents the eight steps in training the mind in Compassion.
- The Conch Shell represents Ultimate Reality.

Compiled by Ven. Bikkshuni Tenzin Kalsang, B.A.

Suggestions by Sangha for improvements are invited. For details about the Buddhist Community, location of temples, etc., please contact:

Ven. Bikkshuni Tenzin Kalsang
Tengye Ling Tibetan Buddhist Centre
50 Beverley Street
Toronto, Ontario   M5T 1X9

Phone: (416) 977-4656
Pager: (416) 600-6648
Fax: (416) 366-9874

THE CHRISTADELPHIANS

FOUNDER

John Thomas (1805-1871) rediscovered the first century apostolic beliefs.

NATURE OF RELIGION

Monotheistic, Christian

SCRIPTURES

The Holy Bible, authorized version, or any reliable translation such as the revised version, revised standard version, etc.

BASIC BELIEFS

- The Bible is the only true message from God and is entirely given by Him. (II Timothy 3:16; 2 Peter 1:21)

- There is only one God, the Father Who created the world and has a great purpose for it. (I Timothy 2:5; Deutoronomy 6:4)

- The Holy Spirit is God's own power, by which He works out His own holy will. (Luke 1:35; Acts 10:38)

- Jesus is the Son of God. He is also Son of man through being born of the virgin Mary. (Matthew 3:17; Galatians 4:4)

- Jesus overcame all temptation and died to save his followers from sin and death. (Hebrew 2:14; Romans 8:3)

- God raised Jesus from the dead. Later, Jesus ascended to heaven, but he will return. (Acts 1:3, 9; Mark 16:19)

- When he returns he will raise and judge the responsible dead and reward immortality to the faithful. (John 5:29; Daniel 12:1, 2)

- Jesus will be King over the restored Kingdom of God in Israel and over the whole world. (Luke 1:30-33; Isaiah 32:17)

- The devil is not a supernatural being but is another name for sin, destroyed only in Christ. (James 1:14, 15; Hebrews 2:14)

- Salvation involves covering from sin through Christ, and freedom from sin and death at his second coming. (Romans 4:13, 21-25; Hebrews 11:6)

- When man dies he ceases to exist. The only hope of new life is by resurrection at Christ's return. (Psalms 146;4; Ecclesiastes 9:5,6)

- Belief in God's Promises about His Kingdom and the work of Jesus Christ is essential. (Acts 8:12; Acts 2:38)

- Repentance and baptism into Christ by water immersion and following Christ in one's daily life are necessary for ultimate salvation. (Mark 16:16; Romans 6:4)

MODE OF WORSHIP

We meet on the first day of the week (Sundays) to worship, receive exhortation and share bread and wine in memory of our Lord.

OTHER WORSHIP ACTIVITIES

- Sunday School Classes - for both children and adults.
- Public Lectures are held regularly for the proclamation of the Gospel message.
- Mid-week Bible Study Classes for further advancement of scriptural knowledge.

- Christadelphian Youth Circle - a Bible Study, recreation and social activity for young people.

STRUCTURE

Each assembly is autonomous. We are a lay community whose members are elected or appointed to serve. All minister without compensation.

DIVISIONS/DENOMINATIONS

The Christadelphian church originates from the Anabaptist, Protestant tradition.

RITUALS

We celebrate a weekly Memorial (Breaking of Bread) Service, and adult baptism.

LAWS

Not applicable

MODE OF DRESS/MODESTY REQUIREMENTS

We do not follow a specific dress code, but modest dress is required.

DIETARY REQUIREMENTS

Not applicable

HOLY DAYS/FESTIVALS

Not applicable

BELIEFS AND PRACTICES REGARDING DEATH

BELIEFS

Death is the complete cessation of life. There is no conscious existence in death. Those who die in faith await the return of Christ and resurrection from the sleep of death.

PRACTICES

Earth burial is most commonly used by Christadelphians, but cremation is chosen by some. It is an individual choice of preference. A funeral service or memorial service is usually conducted by one of the brethren.

SPECIAL RELIGIOUS RITUALS WHICH CAN BE PERFORMED ONLY BY AN AUTHORIZED REPRESENTATIVE OF THIS FAITH

None

SACRED WRITINGS REQUIRED

Not applicable

SACRED OBJECTS REQUIRED

Not applicable

SYMBOLS

Symbols are not used to identify the Christadelphian organization.

PERIODICALS/MAGAZINES

- *The Christadelphian* - monthly
  Birmingham, U.K.

- *Glad Tidings* - monthly
  Solihull, U.K.

- *The Christadelphian Tidings* - monthly
  Detroit, Michigan, U.S.A.

- *Logos* - monthly
  West Beach, South Australia

- *Herald of the coming Age* - quarterly
  West Beach, South Australia

- *The Bible Magazine* - quarterly
  Prince George, B.C., Canada

This chapter was written by:
Mr. Gary Smith

For further information please write to:
The Christadelphians
P.O. Box 21049
84 Lynden Road
Brantford, Ontario
N3R 7W9

CHRISTIANITY

ORIGINS

Christianity is the faith of those who recognize Jesus of Nazareth as the Christ, the Son of God, and accept him as their Saviour and Lord. They affirm that "God so loved the world that He gave His only Son, so that everyone who believes in him shall not perish but may have eternal life." Christianity's beliefs and practices are the result of the experiences of those who knew Jesus during his earthly life and of those since who know him through the grace of the Holy Spirit, given by God to those who put their trust in him. Most Christians believe that in the one God there are three co-equal persons; Father, Son and Holy Spirit - the Holy Trinity.

The name "Christian", meaning "other Christ", was given to Jesus' followers in the first decades of the Christian era, designated on the common calendar as "A.D." - that is, "Anno Domini", meaning "year of the Lord". Christians are believers who seek to model their lives after the example of Jesus, looking forward to a spiritual life after death in the fulfilment of his promise that he has gone to prepare a place for his followers, and will come again to claim his own at the end of time.

Baptism: In most Christian traditions, believers become Church members either by personal profession of faith or by the profession of their families and sponsors on behalf of infants, followed by water Baptism in the name of the Father, Son and Holy Spirit.

Christian Meal: In most denominations members participate in the Christian family meal, known variously as the Lord's Supper, Holy Communion, Holy Eucharist, the Mass or the Divine Liturgy.

THE LIFE AND MINISTRY OF JESUS

Christians believe that God entered human history by sending His only Son into the world to be our Saviour. Jesus' birth was foretold to Mary who accepted God's will that she bear His Son. Many churches commemorate this annually on the Feast of the Annunciation, March 25. Christmas, observed on December 25 (or on January 7 for those churches which use the Julian calendar) is the annual observance of Jesus' birth. Jesus was born in Bethlehem in Judea and grew up in Nazareth in Galilee, the home of his mother and her spouse Joseph. At age thirty, Jesus' three-year ministry began with his baptism in the Jordan River by his cousin John the Baptist, who preached repentance to prepare the way for the coming Messiah. Many of John's followers became Jesus' disciples.

JESUS' TEACHING

Jesus taught publicly, often using stories known as parables. The scriptures tell us that Jesus performed many miracles such as healing, feeding and raising people to life. By word and example he showed what God is like and how life can be lived. He taught that God is love, and that God can be confidently addressed in prayer as "Our Father". He taught his disciples the prayer which begins with those words, known as the Lord's Prayer.

Jesus was called by others the "Son of God" and called himself "Son of Man". He also spoke of himself as "the light of the world", "the resurrection and the life", "the way, the truth and the life". Through his use of symbolic terms for himself such as "the good shepherd" and "the vine", Jesus' disciples learned how he and they related to one another. Jesus gave his followers new life and purpose, but also informed them that they were called to a life of sacrifice and service to others, that they must "take up their crosses and follow him". Jesus chose twelve disciples who became known as Apostles (meaning "sent"). Many Christians recognize them and other faithful followers as Saints. The apostles were commissioned to proclaim the Gospel, the "Good News" of salvation through Jesus Christ, and in his name to call other disciples who would spread the Gospel throughout the world.

HOLY WEEK

In the last week of his ministry Jesus entered Jerusalem in triumph; the event is commemorated on Palm Sunday. Observing the Jewish Passover, on the Thursday he and his disciples ate their last supper together. In preparation, Jesus washed his disciples' feet as an example of the mutual love and service he expected of his followers. Then in the meal ritual he identified the bread with his body and the wine with his blood, commanding them to recall him in this way thereafter. Thus, Christians believe that Jesus instituted the sacred meal rite which many believers have observed ever since on Sundays and often daily, in his memory and in anticipation of the heavenly banquet Jesus promised his followers.

GOOD FRIDAY

After the Last Supper, as he had predicted, Jesus was betrayed, denied and abandoned by his disciples. After his trial, our Saviour was crucified with common criminals on Friday, commemorated annually as Good Friday. His body was hastily buried in a borrowed tomb.

EASTER DAY

On the third morning, some women who were among Jesus' disciples went to dress his body with spices in the proper Jewish custom, but they found the tomb empty. Later Jesus, risen from the dead as he had predicted, appeared to his disciples. Since that day believers have celebrated Christ's Resurrection on Easter Day. Easter does not have a set date, but falls on the first Sunday following the Spring equinox's first full moon.

ASCENSION

During the next forty days the risen Lord revealed himself to many disciples, continuing to prepare them for his departure from the earth, which took place at his Ascension.

PENTECOST OR WHITSUNDAY

On the Feast of Pentecost the assembled disciples experienced the promised reception of God's Holy Spirit, empowering them for the ministry Jesus had entrusted to them. This day, celebrated seven weeks after Easter, is the "birthday" of the Church.

SCRIPTURES AND DOCTRINES

SCRIPTURES

The Apostles and other disciples began to spread the Good News to all who would hear and believe. Paul was a notable convert who became one of the principle Apostles. Letters from Paul and others to groups of Christians helped to provide common shape to the church's formation. After some decades the oral gospel tradition was set in writing by various authors. These writings included the Gospels of Matthew, Mark, Luke and John, becoming part of the Christian Bible's New Testament. The New Testament was also composed of some of the many letters written by church leaders, which became the chapter entitled "Acts".

The early Councils also defined the Christian Bible's contents, accepting as the Old Testament the Jewish scriptures translated from Hebrew into Greek and then into other languages from these two. Christian writings which believers had been willing to die for during the persecutions became the New Testament. The Holy Bible is accepted by Christians as the authoritative word of God.

Christian Churches now co-operate in the translation of the Bible, available in most of the world's languages. In English, best known versions are the one authorized in 1611 by King James of England and modern translations such as the Jerusalem Bible, the New Revised Standard Version, the New English Bible, the New International Version, the New American Bible, Today's English Version (known as the "Good News Bible"), and many others.

DOCTRINE

The early church was plagued by several generations of vigorous persecution, which ended in the year 325 when the Emperor Constantine adopted Christianity as the Roman Empire's official religion. Constantine encouraged Christian community leaders to meet in General or Ecumenical Councils to decide upon matters of faith and practice. Creeds were formulated to define the faith, the best known being the Nicene Creed. It or the baptismal creed known as the Apostles' Creed is regularly recited in the worship services of many churches to this day. Some Churches which did not subscribe to the councils' decisions, such as the Coptic and Armenian Orthodox, are part of the Christian family today.

THE GROWTH OF CHRISTIANITY

Christianity expanded rapidly throughout the Roman Empire and beyond. With the decline of that empire, Christian leadership divided between the Bishop of Rome (the Pope), and the Patriarch of Constantinople. Their followers, the Western (Catholic) and Eastern (Orthodox) Churches formally separated in 1054 AD. In Europe, the 16th century saw several reform movements in the western Church, inspired by theologians such as Martin Luther, John Knox, and John Calvin. The Roman Catholic Church responded with its internal Counter Reformation. The Protestant and Reformed Churches which broke with the Roman Catholic Church sought to recover or stress certain dimensions of Christian Faith and practice. Translating the bible into the people's languages was a central point of these movements, as well as the use of the vernacular in public worship. Some reforms were more jurisdictional than theological, resulting in nationally governed churches. In succeeding centuries movements within denominations have led to the separation of new church bodies with their own distinctive emphasis and practice; others have evolved from the shared faith and experience of individual believers.

In recent years, Christendom is experiencing a great convergence in belief and practice, generating respect and co-operation at all levels of Church life, in local ministerial associations, regional and national coalitions, and in international bodies which promote mutual understanding, peace and world relief.

PASTORAL CARE

In the Christian traditions, pastoral (spiritual and religious) care enables those in need to experience the fullness of life which Jesus gives. It is provided by Christians through such means as:

Counselling: Helping people to make sense out of life experiences and events in the light of God's revelation in Christ.

Visiting: Providing a source of support and comfort in times of special need, such as difficult moral choices, pain, grief and sorrow.

Celebrating: Providing religious services and resources to encourage, inspire and motivate people for life.

Nurturing: Helping people to understand and interpret life in the light of biblical principles and Christian teachings.

Pastoral care is normally provided to church members by qualified persons of the denomination and congregation to which they belong. For those in institutions, pastoral care may be provided by chaplains and volunteers from various Christian bodies, as well as by denominational representatives visiting to provide specific care for their own members.

While most churches co-operate in providing pastoral care to all Christians, respect for the integrity of separate Christian traditions demands that the distinctive means provided by individual denominations to meet the spiritual and religious needs of their members be accessible as required.

The Rev. Tom James
with the co-operation of the other Christian members of
Ontario Multifaith Council on Spiritual and Religious Care.

The succeeding pages outline the characteristics of some denominations, and provide specific information which might be of assistance to chaplains in ensuring appropriate pastoral care to Christians of various traditions.

THE ANGLICAN CHURCH OF CANADA

FOUNDER

The heading "Founder" does not apply to the Anglican Church, which sees itself as a reformed part of the church catholic present in the British Isles from as early as possibly the second century.

NATURE OF RELIGION

Religion is a faith response to the revelation of God. That revelation is acknowledged as the showing forth of God in creation, the Incarnation of God in Jesus Christ and the empowerment of God's people through the gift of the Holy Spirit. The Anglican faith response to this revelation is the acknowledgement of life as essentially sacramental.

SCRIPTURES

Richard Hooker, whose writings at the time of the Elizabethan settlement (ca. 1581) have identified him as the most accomplished advocate of Anglicanism, maintained that Scripture could only be understood in the dual lights of reason and tradition. The Bible is the church's book. The thirty-nine books of the Old Testament and the twenty-seven books of the New Testament, together with the fourteen books of the Apocrypha are the accepted writings for the Church.

BASIC BELIEFS

Christian belief has its origins in the doctrine of creation. The Incarnation of God in our Lord Jesus Christ is the ultimate act of creation. The incarnation of our Lord Jesus Christ is the ultimate act of creation. From this truth we see the whole created order as good. The presence of sin cannot be explained by its identification with the material order. Sin resides in the person and/or the collective, the community. The gift of reason gives rise to the possibility of sin.

> ...the Incarnation embraces the totality of life. It is the doctrine which undergirds the Anglican commitment to sensibility, the openness to the entire experience with all its conflict and ambiguity [Holmes, p.29].

MODE OF WORSHIP

Worship is an act of thanksgiving to Almighty God in which the faithful participate through their union in Christ. The forms of worship for the Anglican Church are found in the Book of Common Prayer and the Book of Alternative Services. Holy Communion, morning and evening prayer form the core of worship in these books. Services for other special occasions have been added.

Individual prayer and Bible reading is also expected as part of a believer's worship.

STRUCTURE

The Anglican Church of Canada is composed of thirty dioceses governed by synods. Each diocese is led by an elected bishop. There are four metropolitan archbishops supervising the four provinces. The Primate of Canada presides over the governing General Synod.

The Anglican Church recognizes three orders of ordained ministry; Bishop, Priest and Deacon. Bishops alone have the power to ordain. Priests share with bishops the responsibility of celebrating the Eucharist, granting absolution of sins, and performing baptisms and marriages.

Lay persons share with priests and deacons the pastoral ministry to parish members. Such persons may be licensed to administer Holy Communion from the sacrament consecrated at the Eucharist, as well as to anoint with blessed oil, and to lay hands on and pray for the sick.

DIVISIONS/DENOMINATIONS

Anglicanism as a doctrinal system has preserved its catholic roots while adapting selective principles of the continental reformation. Division within Anglicanism is found generally within these two schools (catholic and reform), that are held together in a unity that allows a wide diversity of expression.

RITUALS (SACRAMENTS)

Baptism: Christian initiation is by water baptism, normally performed by a priest.

Holy Communion: Most Anglicans receive Holy Communion regularly. This is the principle act of worship on Sundays.

Confession: General confession is part of most worship services; private confession may be made to a priest.

Marriage: Marriage celebrations are normally witnessed and blessed by a priest.

Anointing The Sick: The sick may request anointing with blessed oil.

Anglicans are permitted to receive the ministrations from representatives of any Christian denomination, but should be entitled to receive the Sacraments from Anglican priests or authorized ministers on request, especially if a chaplain is not ordained in a sacramental tradition.

The created order is essentially sacramental. The sacraments are not only signs of God's love and compassion, but convey God's presence to the Church. The theology of the Anglican Church is embodied in its liturgy. Anglicans hold to the guideline "lex orandi, lex credendi", which means "the law of praying is the law of believing".

LAWS

Diocesan and General Synods, the Church's governing bodies, are ordered in accordance with operational canons which address parish administration and church discipline for both clergy and laity.

MODE OF DRESS/MODESTY REQUIREMENTS

Not Applicable

DIETARY REQUIREMENTS

None. Anglicans may choose to observe the discipline of fasting on Fridays and during Lent.

HOLY DAYS/FESTIVALS

Anglicans follow the general holy days of the Christian calendar.

BELIEFS AND PRACTICES REGARDING DEATH

BELIEFS

Jesus Christ's followers share in his victory over death and in the resurrection of the body. The communion of saints binds all Christians, living and dead, together in a spiritual union in Christ.

PRACTICES

Funerals or memorial services are normally conducted in a church.

The use of prayer with the sacrament of unction may be in order in the event of illness. The order is set forward in the Book of Alternative Services, pages 554 to 558. This is followed by a rite Concerning Ministry at the Time of Death, pages 559 to 564. Rubrics indicate that ordained or lay persons may lead in these prayers with consideration being given to presentation by someone with whom the sick person is familiar. The sacrament of unction "...asks that whatever may be the present physical condition of a person, that he or she be open to God's healing love in whatever form and to whatever end it may come." [Holmes, pg. 27]

SPECIAL RELIGIOUS RITUALS WHICH CAN BE PERFORMED ONLY BY AN AUTHORIZED REPRESENTATIVE OF THIS FAITH

Please refer to the section entitled *Rituals (Sacraments),* above.

SACRED WRITINGS REQUIRED

Anglicans use many translations of the Bible. They may also require the Book of Common Prayer of the book of Alternative Services. Requests may be made for the *Book of Common Praise* or the Hymn Book, which hold familiar music.

SACRED OBJECTS REQUIRED

None

SYMBOLS

A great many symbols, depicting in art form the people, places and events in the life of our Lord and the Church's history are used as visual aids to convey our faith in both teaching and architecture.

OTHER BOOKS

The following references provide further details regarding the Anglican Church:

What is Anglicanism? Urban T. Holmes III, Toronto, Ontario: The Anglican Book Centre, 1982. ISBN 0-919030-76-9

This is Our Faith. Ian Stuchbery, Toronto, Ontario: The Anglican Book Centre, 1990. ISBN 0-921846-21-5
- A guide to life and belief for Anglicans with a revised chapter on worship. This is a confirmation manual prepared by a Canadian with particular references to the Canadian Church.

This chapter was written by:
Rev. John Flindall
The Anglican Church of Canada
27 March Street, P.O. Box 419
Frankford, Ontario
K0K 2C0
(613) 398-7219

THE APOSTOLIC CHURCH OF PENTECOST

FOUNDER

The Apostolic Church of Pentecost is a part of the Universal Church which has as its Founder, the Lord Jesus Christ. The Canadian denomination received its charter in 1921. The Reverend Franklin Small of Winnipeg, Manitoba was the founding Moderator.

NATURE OF RELIGION

Monotheistic, Evangelical, Protestant.

SCRIPTURES

The Holy Bible.

BASIC BELIEFS

We believe:

- In the verbal inspiration of the Holy Scriptures.

- In the existence of One True God who has revealed Himself to this world as the Father, as the Son, and as the Holy Spirit.

- In humankind's Saviour, the Lord Jesus Christ, conceived by the Holy Spirit, born of the Virgin Mary, very God and very man.

- In the creation, test and fall of humankind, as recorded in Genesis; its total spiritual depravity and inability to attain divine righteousness.

- In the Gospel of God's Grace, revealed through Christ's death, burial and resurrection on the third day for our justification.

- In Jesus Christ's perfect work upon the cross of Calvary, through which sinners are redeemed by faith alone, in accordance with God's Grace.

- In water baptism of believers, through immersion in the name of our Lord Jesus Christ.

- In Baptism of the Holy Spirit as an experience subsequent to salvation with scriptural evidence; namely, speaking in tongues.

- In the gifts of the Spirit as enumerated in I Corinthians, being exercised and practiced as manifest in the early church.

- In the Lord's supper, as a memorial for believers.

- In the healing of the body by Divine power, or Divine healing in many aspects as practiced by the early church.

- In eternal life for the believer, and eternal punishment for the unbeliever.

- In the expression of Christian faith through a Spirit-filled life, a life of separation from the world, and the perfecting of holiness in the fear of God.

- In the reality and personality of Satan and demons.

- In the reality and ministry of holy angels.

- In the personal return of the Lord Jesus Christ for His church.

MODE OF WORSHIP

Pentecostals worship individually, through scripture reading and communication with the Lord in prayer and praise. We also join together for a public celebration of our faith through congregational worship of prayer, praise and Bible ministry.

STRUCTURE

A Moderator presides over the national office. A Presbyter presides over each district office. Local churches are autonomous in structure and government and presided over by a Pastor. Each office or church may have support staff.

DIVISIONS/DENOMINATIONS

The Apostolic Church of Pentecost is a member of the Pentecostal denomination of the Christian Church.

RITUALS

Pentecostals participate in Christian rituals such as water baptism, the Lord's Supper, infant dedication, marriage ceremonies, and funerals.

LAWS

Not Applicable

MODE OF DRESS/MODESTY REQUIREMENTS

Those taught in scripture consistent with local cultures and Christian practice.

DIETARY REQUIREMENTS

None

HOLY DAYS/FESTIVALS

While not esteeming any day above another, we recognize Sunday as the traditional day for congregational worship, and Christmas, Good Friday, and Easter as days to commemorate Jesus Christ's birth, death, and resurrection respectively.

BELIEFS AND PRACTICES REGARDING DEATH

BELIEFS

We believe in life after death, in the bodily resurrection, and that our eternal destiny is determined by the decisions made in this life as taught in scripture.

PRACTICES

We practice the normal funeral service.

SPECIAL RELIGIOUS RITUALS WHICH CAN BE PERFORMED ONLY BY AN AUTHORIZED REPRESENTATIVE OF THIS FAITH

Our ministers are authorized to perform all Christian rituals such as Water Baptism, marriages and funerals. However, we also recognize the validity of these ceremonies when performed by other Christian ministers or civil authorities.

SACRED WRITINGS REQUIRED

The Holy Bible, both Old and New Testaments, in their various translations.

SACRED OBJECTS REQUIRED

None

SYMBOLS

The Apostolic Church of Pentecost does not use any specific symbols.

SCHOOLS AND INSTITUTIONS

There are two nationally recognized teaching institutions; Full Gospel Bible Institute, Eston, Saskatchewan and Full Gospel Indian Bible School, Fort Qu'appelle, Saskatchewan. Local churches operate Christian education programs and schools. Auxiliary departments operate within churches, such as men, women, youth, missions, etc..

This chapter was written by:
Rev. Joseph O. Moore
814-20 Graydon Hall Drive
Don Mills, Ontario
M3A 3A1
(416) 444-770

THE BAPTIST CHURCH

FOUNDER

Christians who describe themselves as Baptist had their beginnings in the early 17th century. They are an expression of the larger Christian church and would thus claim Jesus Christ as the head and founder of the Church.

NATURE OF RELIGION

Monotheistic, Christian.

SCRIPTURES

The Holy Bible

BASIC BELIEFS

- **The Lordship of Jesus Christ**: Baptists believe that no individual person is head of the church, rather they look to Jesus Christ as head.

- **The Bible is the authoritative word of God**: Baptists believe in following the Bible in all matters of faith and practice.

- **Regenerate Church membership**: Baptists believe that the church comprises those who have personally experienced faith in Jesus Christ. Thus Baptists do not practice the baptism of infants, but rather baptism of believers.

- **Soul Liberty**: Baptists do not accept human dictums which claim to be the official voice of God but rather encourage each individual's right to seek God's lead in all matters.

- **Priesthood of all Believers**: Baptists believe that not only does each individual believer have the right to approach God but that believers are also to act as priests to one another.

MODE OF WORSHIP

On a weekly basis, usually Sunday, Baptists meet together for corporate worship. Individuals are also encouraged to establish their own private worship. This takes the form of Bible reading and personal prayer.

STRUCTURE

The local church is the most important and basic group of Christians. Each individual church is autonomous and not under an outside authority's jurisdiction. However, groups of churches, usually geographically determined, form associations of churches. On a provincial or national level they also form themselves into conventions or unions. Many national unions and conventions affiliate with a world body known as the Baptist World Alliance.

DIVISIONS/DENOMINATIONS

Within Canada there are five major groupings of Baptists, to which most local Baptist churches give their allegiance. They are:

- Baptist Federation of Canada
- Fellowship of Evangelical Baptists
- North American Baptists

- General Conference Baptists
- Southern Baptists of Canada

Across the country there are also individual Baptist churches which prefer to remain independent.

RITUALS (SACRAMENTS)

Baptism and Holy Communion are considered to be the two sacraments that Baptists practice. Immersion Baptism is the means by which a believer publicly proclaims his or her inner experience of faith in Christ. Communion, a sacramental meal, is usually practiced once or twice per month.

LAWS

Not Applicable

MODE OF DRESS/MODESTY REQUIREMENTS

Not Applicable

DIETARY REQUIREMENTS

Not Applicable

HOLY DAYS/FESTIVALS

The two main Holy seasons recognized by most Baptists are Christmas and Easter. Christmas Day is the celebration of Jesus Christ's birth. Easter (Good Friday and Easter Sunday), is the celebration of Jesus Christ's crucifixion and resurrection.

BELIEFS AND PRACTICES REGARDING DEATH

Not   Applicable

SPECIAL RELIGIOUS RITUALS WHICH CAN BE PERFORMED ONLY BY AN AUTHORIZED REPRESENTATIVE OF THIS FAITH

A distinctive Baptist belief is the "priesthood of all believers". From this belief we derive the concept that a person who performs a particular ministry may have a different function but not a different status from any other Christian. Thus, in theory, any believer can perform any function within the life of a Baptist church. In practice, usually an "ordained person" (one set aside for a particular function) performs marriages and conducts funeral services.

SACRED WRITINGS REQUIRED

The Holy Bible is the one book considered to be God's revelation, and is used as God's Word in all matters of faith and practice. Hymnbooks are used but vary greatly from one church to another, and are not considered to be sacred in the same sense as the Holy Bible.

SACRED OBJECTS REQUIRED

Not Applicable

SYMBOLS

Baptists tend to emphasize Christian faith as an "inner experience" and thus tend not to emphasize the external, especially symbols. However, symbols do appear within churches. The most common symbol is the empty cross - reminding people of Jesus Christ's sacrificial death for them, as well as the fact that Jesus Christ has risen and is no longer on the cross. The Communion table, symbolizing the meal Jesus had with His disciples prior to His death, is a symbolic piece of furniture found in most Baptist churches.

SCHOOLS AND INSTITUTIONS

Seminaries are established to train pastors who are responsible for giving leadership in pastoral care, preaching and the administering of the church. Seminary training is usually a post graduate course of study which takes two to three years to complete.

This chapter was written by:
Rev. John A. Wilton
The Baptist Convention of Ontario and Quebec
195 The West Mall, Suite 414
Etobicoke, Ontario
M9C 5K1
(416) 622-8600

THE CANADIAN CONFERENCE BRETHREN IN CHRIST CHURCH

FOUNDER

Believers in the Anabaptist tradition began meetings around 1778 in Pennsylvania. By 1788, several families moved to Southern Ontario (Fonthill/ Fort Erie). The first bishop in Ontario was John Winger.

NATURE OF RELIGION

Monotheistic, Christian, Trinitarian

SCRIPTURES

The Old and New Testaments of the Christian Church.

BASIC BELIEFS

- God as Father, Son, and Holy Spirit is revealed through nature and through the Christian scriptures.

- God is the creator of all life; man and woman are created in His image.

- Humans chose to disobey God, becoming alienated from God, from one another, from themselves and from the rest of creation.

- Jesus the Christ came to earth as God the Son, to provide the plan of salvation for all humanity.

- Personal faith in the sacrificial death and resurrection of Jesus Christ brings one into new life in Christ. This restores the broken relationships referred to above.

- The universal Christian church is God's primary means of spreading the good news of Jesus Christ around the world.

MODE OF WORSHIP

Church members participate in group worship on Sundays, consisting of singing, scripture readings, prayers, sermons and offerings. Individual and family devotions are encouraged daily.

STRUCTURE

The Canadian Conference Brethren In Christ Church conducts its business in an annual one-day session. The moderator is the assigned bishop. Several standing committees oversee assigned ministries. Each congregation has one or more pastors, with a church board of deacons/lay members. The Canadian conference functions as part of the North American General Conference.

DIVISIONS/DENOMINATIONS

The Canadian Conference Brethren in Christ Church is a branch of the Anabaptist tradition, an evangelical, Protestant denomination of the Christian Church. It is a member of the Mennonite Central Committee.

RITUALS

Baptism: Water baptism is by complete immersion, kneeling forward in submission to Christ.

Holy Communion: Holy Communion is observed quarterly in the congregations.

LAWS

We follow the ten commandments, and the New Testament law of love for one another.

MODE OF DRESS/MODESTY REQUIREMENTS

Modesty and simplicity are taught.

DIETARY REQUIREMENTS

Food - none. Use of alcoholic beverages is not accepted.

HOLY DAYS/FESTIVALS

We follow the general holy days of the Christian calendar.

BELIEFS AND PRACTICES REGARDING DEATH

BELIEFS

The believer is welcomed through Jesus Christ directly into God's presence, unto everlasting blessing. The unbeliever is separated from God unto everlasting condemnation.

PRACTICES

Cultural practices of embalming, funeral ceremonies and cremation are accepted.

SPECIAL RELIGIOUS RITUALS WHICH CAN BE PERFORMED ONLY BY AN AUTHORIZED REPRESENTATIVE OF THIS FAITH

Most Christian rituals should be performed by an ordained pastor. These include baptism, marriage and funeral ceremonies.

SACRED WRITINGS REQUIRED

The Holy Bible. Our members also use *Hymns For Praise and Worship*, (1984).

SACRED OBJECTS REQUIRED

None

SYMBOLS

The central symbols are the cross, the dove, and a basin and towel.

This chapter was written by:
Rev. Leonard Chester
Canadian Conference Brethren in Christ Church
5384 Sherkston Road
Sherkston, Ontario
L0S 1R0
(905) 894-0673

THE CHRISTIAN AND MISSIONARY ALLIANCE

FOUNDER

The Christian and Missionary Alliance was founded by Dr. A.B. Simpson, a Canadian of Presbyterian background, who before founding this worldwide movement had pastored successful Churches in Canada and the U.S.A.

NATURE OF RELIGION

Monotheistic, Christian

SCRIPTURES

Members of the Christian and Missionary Alliance use many translations of the Bible, most commonly the New International Version or the Authorized King James Version.

BASIC BELIEFS

The following is the Statement of Faith as adopted by the Denomination:

There is one God, who is infinitely perfect, existing eternally in three persons; Father, Son, and Holy Spirit.

Jesus Christ is true God and true man. He was conceived by the Holy Spirit and born of the Virgin Mary. He died upon the cross, the Just for the unjust, as a substitutionary sacrifice, and all who believe in Him are justified on the grounds of His shed blood. He arose from the dead according to the Scriptures. He is now at the right hand of the Majesty on high as our great High Priest. He will come again to establish His kingdom of righteousness and peace.

The Holy Spirit is a divine person, sent to indwell, guide, teach and empower the believer, and to convince the world of sin, righteousness and judgment.

The Old and New Testaments, inerrant as originally given, were verbally inspired by God and are a complete revelation of His will for the salvation of humankind. They constitute the divine and only rule of Christian faith and practice.

Humankind was originally created in the image and likeness of God, then fell through disobedience, thereby incurring both physical and spiritual death. All people are born with a sinful nature, are separated from the life of God, and can be saved only through the atoning work of the Lord Jesus Christ. The portion of the unrepentant and unbelieving is existence forever in conscious torment; that of the believer, in everlasting joy and bliss.
Salvation has been provided through Jesus Christ for all people, and those who repent and believe in Him are born again of the Holy Spirit, receive the gift of eternal life, and become the children of God.

It is God's will that each believer should be filled with the Holy Spirit and be sanctified wholly, separated from sin and the world and fully dedicated to the will of God, thereby receiving power for holy living and effective service. This is both a crisis and a progressive experience wrought in the believer's life subsequent to conversion.

The Lord Jesus Christ provides redemption and healing of the mortal body. Prayer for the sick and anointing with oil are taught in the Scriptures and are privileges for the Church in this present age.

The Church consists of all those who believe in the Lord Jesus Christ, are redeemed through His blood (shed in His sacrifice on the cross), and are born again of the Holy Spirit. Christ is the Head of the Body, the Church, whom He has commissioned to go into the world as a witness, preaching the Gospel to all nations.

The local church is a body of believers in Christ, who are joined together for the worship of God, for edification through the Word of God, for prayer, fellowship, the proclamation of the Gospel, and observance of the ordinances of Baptism and the Lord's Supper.

There shall be a bodily resurrection of the just and the unjust; for the former, a resurrection unto life; for the latter, a resurrection unto judgment.

The second coming of the Lord Jesus Christ is imminent and will be personal, visible, and premillennial. This is the believer's blessed hope and is a vital truth which is an incentive to holy living and faithful service.

MODE OF WORSHIP

Sunday worship services, singing, prayer, bible reading and teaching.

STRUCTURE

The Christian and Missionary Alliance in Canada is governed by a General Assembly which is composed of licensed workers and lay representatives from local churches. It meets every two years.

Canada is divided into geographic Districts, each governed by a District Conference which is also composed of licensed workers and lay representatives from local churches. Each District Conference elects a District Superintendent who provides oversight to the District. The Province of Ontario is under the jurisdiction of the Eastern and Central Canadian District. In 1995, Ontario will be divided into two Districts. This division roughly draws a line from north to south, skirting the Eastern shore of Lake Simcoe.

The Christian and Missionary Alliance ordains those who are called to a preaching and theological ministry. Their titles reflect their role in the local church. Ordained clergy are usually called Pastors.

Lay persons share with Pastors in the ministry to members of local churches, including administrations, teaching and caring ministries.

DIVISIONS/DENOMINATIONS

The Christian and Missionary Alliance in Canada is an autonomous part of the Alliance World Fellowship, consisting of Christian and Missionary Alliance National Church groups in over fifty countries. The Christian and Missionary Alliance is an Evangelical Protestant denomination with its roots in the holiness revivals of the late 1800's.

RITUALS

Baptism:	Christian initiation is achieved through water baptism by immersion. Baptism is normally, but not necessarily, performed by a pastor.
Holy Communion:	Most members receive Holy Communion at least monthly.
Marriage:	Marriage celebrations are conducted by pastors.
Care of the Sick:	The sick may request anointing with oil.

LAWS

Behavioural laws are not legislated. The church believes in biblical morality.

MODE OF DRESS/MODESTY REQUIREMENTS

No dress codes; modesty expected.

DIETARY REQUIREMENTS

None

HOLY DAYS/FESTIVALS

The Christian and Missionary Alliance follows general holy days of the Christian calendar.

BELIEFS AND PRACTICES REGARDING DEATH

BELIEFS

Please refer to "Statement of Faith" in the section entitled *Basic Beliefs*, above.

PRACTICES

Funerals are conducted by pastors.

SPECIAL RELIGIOUS RITUALS WHICH CAN BE PERFORMED ONLY BY AN AUTHORIZED REPRESENTATIVE OF THIS FAITH

Ordinations of pastors, licensing of workers, wedding ceremonies.

SACRED WRITINGS REQUIRED

In addition to a Bible, Church members may request a hymn book and Bible study materials.

SACRED OBJECTS REQUIRED

Not Applicable.

SYMBOLS

The emblem of The Christian and Missionary Alliance consists of four symbols representing the centrality of Christ in a fourfold manner:

- The Cross stands for salvation through the death and resurrection of Jesus Christ, God's son.

- The Laver is representative of sanctification, daily cleansing from sin by the power of the indwelling Holy Spirit.

- The Pitcher speaks of oil for divine life and physical healing made possible through Christ's provision in His atonement.

- The Crown symbolizes the return of our Lord Jesus Christ as King of Kings and Lord of Lords.

SCHOOLS AND INSTITUTIONS

Denominational training is provided at Canadian Bible College/Canadian Theological Seminary in Regina, Saskatchewan.

This chapter was written by:
Rev. Gordon Bucek
Assistant to the Superintendent
Christian and Missionary Alliance
155 Panin Road
Burlington, Ontario
L7V 1A1
(905) 639-9615

THE CHRISTIAN REFORMED CHURCH

FOUNDER

The Christian Reformed Church was born and rooted in the Reformation.

NATURE OF RELIGION

Monotheistic, Reformed Christian

SCRIPTURES

The Holy Bible

BASIC BELIEFS

All of life is religion, and the Bible is the only rule of faith. The denomination adheres to the ecumenical creeds and to three Reformed confessions.

MODE OF WORSHIP

Congregations vary in their mode of worship.

STRUCTURE

The church follows the Presbyterian principle of church government. Local boards are called Councils. The Councils delegate to Classes, and the Classes delegate four persons to the annual Synod.

DIVISIONS/DENOMINATIONS

The church is a reformed, Protestant denomination. We have Canadian and American divisions. The Canadian office is located in Burlington, Ontario.

RITUALS

The denomination observes two Sacraments; baptism and the Last Supper. Only ordained clergy administer the sacraments.

LAWS

The Christian Reformed Church adheres to general Christian morals and principles.

MODE OF DRESS/MODESTY REQUIREMENTS

None

DIETARY REQUIREMENTS

None

HOLY DAYS/FESTIVALS

The denomination follows the church calendar, observing especially Advent and Lent. All Christian holy days are celebrated.

BELIEFS AND PRACTICES REGARDING DEATH

BELIEFS

As stated in the Apostolic Creed, "...we believe in the resurrection of the body, and the life everlasting".

PRACTICES

The denomination holds funeral services, at which ordained ministers usually, but not necessarily officiate.

SPECIAL RELIGIOUS RITUALS WHICH CAN BE PERFORMED ONLY BY AN AUTHORIZED REPRESENTATIVE OF THIS FAITH

Only ordained clergy administer the sacraments.

SACRED WRITINGS REQUIRED

The Bible

SACRED OBJECTS REQUIRED

None

SYMBOLS

The denomination uses a wide variety of Christian symbols.

SCHOOLS AND INSTITUTIONS

The denomination operates both Calvin College and Calvin Seminary in Grand Rapids, MI.

SUMMARY

As the official name implies, the Christian Reformed Church is an international denomination. There are Canadian and American wings to the faith group. The Canadian office is located in Burlington, Ontario while the American wing has its administrative offices in Grand Rapids, Michigan. The Council of Christian Reformed Churches in Canada meets at different national locations every other year, to regulate the national interest of the Canadian congregations. The international assembly called the Synod, meets annually. The denomination follows the Presbyterian model of church government.

The C.R.C. in North America was born as a result of a series of secessions from what is probably the oldest Protestant denomination on the American continent; the Reformed Church of America. The first of these secessions took place in the Netherlands in 1834.

The first seceders moved to America in 1847 to establish a colony in western Michigan. As early as possible the settlers met in an ecclesiastical assembly. The first meeting was held in the Michigan village of Zeeland in 1848. These meetings resulted in the beginning of a new ecclesiastical fellowship. The Christian Reformed Church began its existence on April 8, 1857.

From its very beginning to present day, certain elements characterize the denomination, namely its desire to continue the historic standards and creeds of the Reformation. Along with the ecumenical creeds the denomination adheres and subscribes to the Heidelberg Catechism, the Canons of Dort and the Belgic Confession. To these creedal standards the church has recently added a contemporary testimony entitled, *Our World Belongs to God.*

The faith group is distinguished still by an intense interest in theology. One of its foundational considerations is that all of life is religion. This world and life view expresses that regardless of one's sphere or life activity, one's attitude is determined and defined by his or her religious beliefs and convictions.

The denomination's members apply this principle especially, but not exclusively, to education. In addition to its Calvin Theological Seminary, the church operates numerous other institutions of learning, from elementary schools to colleges. Two of these colleges are located in Canada; King's College in Edmonton, Alberta and Redeemer College in Hamilton, Ontario.

The Christian Reformed Church maintains ecclesiastical fellowship with many other denominations, among which are many Christian Reformed Churches in other countries. It has also established a special warm relationship with the Reformed Church of America from which it seceded a century ago.

Currently, the denomination counts 978 congregations, with a total membership of 300,320. A slight annual growth continues to expand its membership.

This chapter was written by:
Rev. Carl D. Tuyl
The Christian Reformed Church

Canadian Office:
    3475 Mainway, P.O. Box 5070
    Burlington, Ontario
    L7R 3Y8
    (905) 336-2920
    Fax: (905) 336-8344
    Charitable Registration No. 0590018-49

American Office:
    2850 Kalamazoo Avenue, SE
    Grand Rapids, Michigan
    49560
    (616) 246-0744
    Fax: (616) 246-0834

THE EVANGELICAL LUTHERAN CHURCH IN CANADA

FOUNDER

On October 31, 1517, Martin Luther posted on the chapel door in Wittenberg, Germany, 95 theses (statements) questioning various church practices. This is traditionally considered the beginning of the "Protestant Reformation" and the Lutheran Church.

NATURE OF RELIGION

Lutherans are monotheistic and Christian, believing in One God manifested in three persons; Father, Son and Holy Spirit.

SCRIPTURES

Lutherans confess the Hebrew and Christian Scriptures of the Bible to be the Word of God and the basis for Lutheran belief, teaching and activity in life.

BASIC BELIEFS

Lutherans believe in a loving God that calls people to faith in Jesus Christ and sends them into the world on a mission. The body of believers is a community called the Church. It is by the Holy Spirit's power that this community is created and sustained in its mission and service to the world. These basic beliefs are stated in the *Augsburg Confession* and in Martin Luther's *Small Catechism*.

MODE OF WORSHIP

Lutherans believe in the importance of regular worship. Preaching and teaching of God's Word and administering the sacraments of Holy Baptism and Holy Communion (the Eucharist) are central to Lutheran worship. Together these are the *Means of Grace* for sustaining Lutheran Christians in the community, providing forgiveness of sins, and sustaining new life of discipleship and hope for the ultimate resurrection of life in the world to come.

STRUCTURE

The Evangelical Lutheran Church in Canada (ELCIC) is one of 2 independent Lutheran churches in Canada. It was formed in 1986 through the union of the Lutheran Church in America (Canadian Section), and the Evangelical Lutheran Church of Canada. The ELCIC is a member of the Lutheran World Federation, a worldwide communion of some 104 Lutheran churches.

The ELCIC is comprised of 5 regional synods, each with a Bishop elected to a 4 year term, and has a national office in Winnipeg, with a national bishop similarly elected for a 4 year term. The Church meets every 2 years in convention to determine policy and elect officers (Bishop, Vice President/Chairperson, Treasurer, Secretary). Between conventions, the national Church Council and the Synod Councils govern the Church.

There is only one ordained ministry to word and sacrament in the ELCIC. Bishops ordain pastors on behalf of the Church after completing a 3 year period of theological study, successfully completing a supervised internship, and successfully passing the examining committee of the Church. Bishops are elected every 4 years and are installed by the Church to a ministry of oversight.

DIVISIONS/DENOMINATIONS

There are 2 major Lutheran denominations in Canada; The Evangelical Lutheran Church in Canada (ELCIC) with 207,000 members (1993) and the Lutheran Church - Canada (LC-C) with 93,000 members (1993). Ninety-six percent of all Lutherans in Canada belong to these 2 denominations. There are a number of smaller Lutheran denominations as well.

While very distinct in their approaches, the ELCIC and LC-C engage in very modest co-operation in relief and development work through Canadian Lutheran World Relief (CLWR), in providing military chaplains federally through the Federal Interfaith Committee, and in theological discussions through the Lutheran Council in Canada.

One crucial distinction is that the ELCIC actively participates in ecumenical and multifaith organizations while the LC-C has not participated regularly.

RITUALS

Lutherans believe in two sacraments, Baptism and Holy Communion. Additionally we follow six rites; Private Confession, Confirmation, Marriage, Ordination, Commendation of the Dying and Burial of the Dead. Lutherans practice both public confession in a general order of confession and private confession with an ordained pastor to confess specific sins that trouble the conscience. An ordained pastor administers the sacraments, except in extreme emergencies. Normally an ordained pastor also presides at rites. Clergical ministers are also needed for marriage which involves a legal function on behalf of the province, usually requiring a provincial license.

Lutherans are permitted to participate in ecumenical worship services and receive the sacraments from other Christian churches who share a similar confessional basis (those who follow the Apostle's, Nicene, and Athanasian Creeds). Pastors are also encouraged to visit other churches and to administer the sacraments, teach, console and to hear confession among those unable to actively participate in the worshipping community's life.

LAWS

Lutherans are expected to follow Jesus Christ's teachings and his commandment to love another.

MODE OF DRESS/MODESTY REQUIREMENTS

Clergy very often wear clerical collars as a sign of their office. In general worship, clergy will wear vestments (albs and stoles, cassocks, chasubles for the Eucharist). Lay persons do not follow a dress code.

DIETARY REQUIREMENTS

There are no special dietary requirements. However, some Lutherans elect to fast during Lent in the pre-Easter season that remembers Christ's suffering.

HOLY DAYS/FESTIVALS

Lutherans follow the general holy days of the Christian calendar. Particularly important days are Christmas, Ash Wednesday, Good Friday and Easter.

BELIEFS AND PRACTICES REGARDING DEATH

BELIEFS

Lutherans believe in the "...resurrection of the dead and the life of the world to come." While death is not to be desired, neither is death a cause for fear and dread, because God promises everlasting life to believers in Jesus Christ.

PRACTICES

As death approaches, Lutherans often request private communion which involves confession. In some cases, Lutherans may request the "commendation of the Dying", also known as "last rites". These are normally provided by ordained clergy.

After death occurs, pastors usually conduct a funeral service which may take a variety of forms, depending upon the wishes of the deceased's family and friends. In its simplest form it may be a memorial service without the body present, a service for the Burial of the Dead, or a full service which includes the Burial of the Dead, a service of the Word and a celebration of the Eucharist (Holy Communion). In the case of the latter two, the body may or may not be present as requested by the individual's family and friends. In some cases, Lutherans have prearranged their funeral services and their wishes should be honoured. Normally, services for members are conducted in a church but they may also be conducted in other settings such as a funeral home, chapel, etc.. It is also appropriate for the Pastor to conduct a committal service at the grave side.

In the months following death, Pastors are available to provide counselling to friends and family.

SPECIAL RELIGIOUS RITUALS WHICH CAN BE PERFORMED ONLY BY AN AUTHORIZED REPRESENTATIVE OF THIS FAITH

An ordained Lutheran Pastor is required to perform most religious rites or rituals. These include Baptism, Catechetical Instruction, Confession, Communion, Commendation of the Dying, Service for Burial of the Dead, and Marriage. In extreme situations, these services may be provided by lay persons, excepting marriage in which a pastor also serves a civil function under the law. Lutheran clergy also co-operate with other denominations in providing these services in some circumstances.

SACRED WRITINGS REQUIRED

Along with the Hebrew and Christian Scriptures, Lutherans may find helpful *Luther's Small Catechism* and the *Lutheran Book of Worship*.

SACRED OBJECTS REQUIRED

Lutherans would find many symbols of the faith, such as crosses and crucifixes and various art, helpful in their spiritual practice. Particularly important is the bread and wine of Holy Communion. Oil for the Commendation of the Dying may also be important.

SYMBOLS

Symbols are important in the Lutheran faith. Please refer to the section entitled *Sacred Objects Required* directly above, for a more detailed description of symbols.

SCHOOLS AND INSTITUTIONS

The ELCIC has 2 seminaries for training ordination candidates and providing continuing education in biblical studies, theology, pastoral counselling and preaching. These seminaries are Waterloo Lutheran Seminary in Waterloo, Ontario and the Lutheran Theological Seminary in Saskatoon, Saskatchewan. In addition, the ELCIC operates 2 colleges and 2 bible colleges in western Canada. The ELCIC also has a number of nursing homes and long term care facilities as well as social service agencies which are owned and operated by the regional synods or local congregations.

This chapter was written by:
Rev. David Pfrimmer
Evangelical Lutheran Church in Canada (Eastern Synod)
The Institute for Christian Ethics
c/o Waterloo Lutheran Seminary
75 University Avenue West
Waterloo, Ontario
N2L 3C5
(519) 884-1970 ext. 2907

THE MENNONITE CHURCH

ORIGIN (FOUNDER)

Mennonites are Christians who trace their roots to the Radical Wing of the sixteenth century's Protestant Reformation. Early leaders, including Menno Simons of the Netherlands to whom the denomination owes its name, believed in a Christian community patterned after the early church and composed of people who freely chose to become members of a voluntary church of believers. They practised believers' baptism rather than the more common infant baptism of the state churches.

Currently Mennonites are a diverse people who speak at least 78 languages and are spread throughout many countries of the world. The movement began among urban professional people. After intense persecution they went through a period when they were almost exclusively rural and often known as "the quiet in the land". However, today they are again predominantly urban in most parts of the world and have entered many professions, the arts, business and even politics.

NATURE OF RELIGION

Monotheistic, Protestant Christian.

SCRIPTURES

The Jewish (Hebrew) Scriptures and the Christian New Testament.

BASIC BELIEFS

Mennonites adhere to basic Christian beliefs. It is their understanding that the Holy Spirit enables Christians to live according to Jesus' personal example and teachings, particularly as described in the Sermon on the Mount. They see Jesus' way of non-resistant love as intrinsic to the gospel, and so refuse to participate in the military. Mennonites commit themselves to living in peaceful, non-violent relationships with others.

MODE OF WORSHIP

As part of the free church tradition, Mennonites are essentially a non-liturgical people whose worship patterns include plenty of spirited singing, scripture readings and prayers, and a biblically-based message which attempts to make scripture relevant in our time. Opportunity is frequently provided as well for sharing of personal concerns with the gathered community.

STRUCTURE

A credentialled pastor ministers in each congregation and is accountable to the Leadership Commission of the Regional Conference.

Lay and ordained persons share in the pastoral ministry to members of their congregations. Mennonites are open to receiving ministry from representatives of any Christian faith. Usually however, local congregation members will actively provide pastoral care when one of their fellow members is hospitalized or a death occurs.

DIVISIONS/DENOMINATIONS

Mennonites are a Protestant denomination of the Christian church.

RITUALS

Mennonites practice the following religious rites:

Water Baptism: Mennonites practice believers' baptism in the context of the local congregation and normally after an instruction period. Water baptism is a symbol of the person's individual response to God's grace, and commitment to a life that demonstrates one is a follower of Jesus Christ and a member of Christ's visible body on earth, the church. Children need not be baptized as they receive God's grace until the age when they are able to make personal decisions to accept the church's faith as their own.

Holy Communion: The Lord's Supper (Communion) is normally served several times a year by both lay and ordained people within the context of the congregation. Mennonites who request Communion outside of the gathered congregation are encouraged to invite several people from the faith community to share the Lord's Supper with them.

Anointing the Sick: The sick may request prayers and anointing with oil and may wish to invite a few persons from their congregation to participate.

LAWS

Not Applicable

MODE OF DRESS/MODESTY REQUIREMENTS

Not Applicable

DIETARY REQUIREMENTS

Not Applicable

HOLY DAYS/FESTIVALS

Christmas, Good Friday and Easter have traditionally been occasions of celebration within the Mennonite faith. Currently, some Mennonite congregations are moving toward a fuller observance of the Church year's celebrations within their worship services.

BELIEFS AND PRACTICES REGARDING DEATH

BELIEFS

Immortality of the soul.

PRACTICES

Not Applicable

SPECIAL RELIGIOUS RITUALS WHICH CAN BE PERFORMED ONLY BY AN AUTHORIZED REPRESENTATIVE OF THIS FAITH

Water Baptism

SACRED WRITINGS REQUIRED

Mennonites use many translations of the bible, and may on occasion request other types of inspirational reading.

SACRED OBJECTS REQUIRED

Not Applicable

SYMBOLS

Not Applicable

This chapter was written by:
Ms. Mary Burkholder
The Mennonite Church of Eastern Canada
4489 King Street East
Kitchener, Ontario
N2G 3W6
(519) 650-3806

THE PENTECOSTAL ASSEMBLIES OF CANADA

FOUNDER

The Pentecostal Assemblies of Canada (PAOC) was formed in 1919 in response to a revival of the ministry of the Holy Spirit that spread across Canada. At this time twenty new congregations formed the nucleus of the movement. Pentecostalism arose from Holiness roots, but embraced a distinctive doctrine that the spirit's fullness is physically manifested by speaking in a new, spirit given language. The Biblical basis for this teaching is taken from a number of texts primarily found in Acts chapters 2, 8, 10 and 19, but also includes Old Testament prophecies such as Joel 2:28ff. Other New testament references include I Corinthians 12-14 and Ephesians 5:18ff.

Thus, the founder of the PAOC is the Spirit of God himself and the church seeks to follow New Testament teaching in a very devout and personal way.

NATURE OF RELIGION

Monotheistic, Christian. Pentecostals look upon the word "religion" with some contempt. We prefer to speak of "relationship". Thus "spirituality" more accurately describes how we see ourselves as opposed to "a religion".

The basis of our spirituality is salvation through Jesus Christ's death and resurrection. Salvation cannot be earned, it can only be accepted. We believe that anyone who rejects Christ as Saviour has rebelled against God and is thus bound for eternal separation from God in Hell.

The practice of Christian living from a Pentecostal perspective places the emphasis on substance over form. That is, we do not believe membership in a church equates with salvation; only sincere, genuine faith and obedience confirms our commitment to Christ.

SCRIPTURES

We believe in the authority and divine inspiration of the Holy Bible. It is the standard by which all decisions, positions and behaviour is judged. while we take a literal view of the Bible, that does not imply a simplistic or wooden interpretation. Rather, it means we treat each genre of Scripture as it has been passed on to us. For example, we treat Old Testament Prophetic writings as a particular genre that demands particular treatment and contextual recognition.

Likewise, Paul's letters are treated in a different contextual light. We apply accepted principles of interpretation such as cultural background, language dynamics, context, and discovery of the author's intention. However, we also affirm the consistency and continuity of all Scripture, since God is its ultimate author.

BASIC BELIEFS

- Humankind is born into "Original Sin". We are separated from our creator by our sin.
- God has a plan of redemption that enables our sin to be forgiven without violating the intrinsic justice and Holiness of God.
- This plan of redemption is based upon Jesus Christ's substitutionary death on our behalf. He gave his life as a ransom for each of us.
- Thus, Jesus is the Saviour of the world - of all peoples of all cultures and customs.

There is no other way to God than through his Son Jesus Christ.

- Pentecostals believe that Jesus Christ is coming back to the earth one day to gather his church unto himself. This is the church's great hope. This is not a hope only for Pentecostals. In fact, our denominational label is completely irrelevant to Christ. He is concerned about the object of our faith. If Christ is our Lord and Saviour, then we are his children. If a religious body or institution is the object of our faith, then the day Jesus returns will be one of disappointment.

- Pentecostals believe in the gift of the Holy Spirit's fullness to all who invite him. When received, this gift is marked by the utterance of new languages or "tongues".

- Heaven is reserved for God's people who have served him faithfully on earth. Hell is the place where those who reject Christ will spend eternity.

MODE OF WORSHIP

Worship is characterized by free and spontaneous singing, praising, clapping and lifting of hands. These gestures can also be punctuated by supernatural gifts of the spirit such as prophecy, a word of knowledge or a prompting to prayer for someone or something. Traditional hymns and scripture readings are common. Preaching of the Scriptures is central to every worship service. Informal gatherings usually include a "Bible study".

Communion is normally conducted monthly although there is no objection to a more frequent observance if desired. Communion is not a means of salvation, but the worshipper's affirmation of his or her commitment to serve Christ and obey his teaching.

STRUCTURE

The PAOC has a national office located in Mississauga, Ontario that administrates the activities of World Missions, ministerial training facilities (Bible Colleges), and specialized departments such as Youth, Seniors, and Men's and Women's groups.

There are seven districts in nine provinces. Newfoundland has remained a separate entity but has close ties with the PAOC, especially in regard to World Missions and Bible Colleges.

Each church elects its Pastor by congregational vote. The PAOC follows the approach of "a fellowship of autonomous churches" that cooperates on matters of missions and theological training. This practice is partially due to a desire to avoid the institutionalization of faith.

DIVISIONS/DENOMINATIONS

The Pentecostal church is an Evangelical, Protestant denomination of the Christian church, which emphasizes gifts of the Holy Spirit. We are part of the worldwide Pentecostal movement, which comprises the largest denomination of the Protestant church.

RITUALS

Salvation has been provided for all humankind through Christ's sacrifice upon the cross. Those who repent and believe in Christ are born again of the Holy Spirit and receive eternal life.

Holy Communion:	The Lord's Supper is a symbol and proclamation of the suffering and death of Christ. This ordinance of communion, normally presided over by a pastor of a local assembly, is to be participated in by believers until Christ's return.
Baptism:	Water baptism signifies the believer's identification with Christ in His death, burial and resurrection and is practiced by immersion. This ordinance is normally presided over by a pastor of a local assembly.
Marriage:	Marriage ceremonies are conducted by an ordained minister.
Anointing the Sick:	The sick may request anointing with oil and the laying on of hands for healing.

LAWS

Pentecostals follow the Ten Commandments and subscribe to the teaching of the entire Bible.

MODE OF DRESS/MODESTY REQUIREMENTS

Not Applicable

DIETARY REQUIREMENTS

None

HOLY DAYS/FESTIVALS

Pentecostals follow Christian holidays; specifically Christmas Day, Good Friday and Easter Sunday.

BELIEFS AND PRACTICES REGARDING DEATH

BELIEFS

We believe that upon death the soul leaves the body to go to heaven. Upon Christ's return, there will be a resurrection of the body and then an ascension to Heaven for rewards and judgement. Those who accepted Christ will enter Heaven, while those who did not serve Christ on earth will be banished to torment in Hell.

PRACTICES

We perform basic Christian funerals, complete with singing and gospel preaching. If the deceased was a believer, we discuss how death's sting is removed because eternal life is found in Christ. This is not intended to diminish the grief over losing a friend or loved one, but simply to offer hope and comfort.

SPECIAL RELIGIOUS RITUALS WHICH CAN BE PERFORMED ONLY BY AN AUTHORIZED REPRESENTATIVE OF THIS FAITH

- As previously mentioned, marriage ceremonies are conducted by an ordained pastor.
- A pastor normally presides at burials, funerals or memorial services which may or may not be conducted in a church.
- Holy Communion is administered by a pastor.

SACRED WRITINGS REQUIRED

The Holy Bible

SACRED OBJECTS REQUIRED

Not Applicable

SYMBOLS

Symbols do not play a significant role in our faith.

This chapter was written by:
Rev. Fred Penney
Pentecostal Assemblies of Canada
Harvest Pentecostal Assembly
Box 521
Don Mills, Ontario
M3C 2T4
(416) 730-1967

THE POLISH CATHOLIC CHURCH

Please refer to the chapter on the Roman Catholic Church

For more information, contact:
Father Jan Rudzewicz
Our Lady Queen of Poland Mission
79 Fredbland Crescent
Scarborough, Ontario
M1J 3L7
(416) 289-0505

74

THE PRESBYTERIAN CHURCH IN CANADA

FOUNDER

Presbyterians regard themselves as part of the universal church founded by Jesus Christ. More specifically, we belong to the Reformed Protestant tradition, tracing our roots back to John Calvin (Geneva) and John Knox (Scotland) in the sixteenth century.

NATURE OF RELIGION

Monotheistic, Christian and Trinitarian.

SCRIPTURES

The Holy Bible, both Old and New Testaments. Its role in our denomination is central; it is God's *written* word, illuminating Jesus Christ, God's *living* word.

BASIC BELIEFS

God is creator of all, eternal and loving. Human beings have sinned; they have broken away from their relationship with God. Jesus Christ is God's Son, both human and divine. He died for our sins, and his resurrection has conquered sin. Christians experience this salvation from sin through trust in Christ. The Holy Spirit is God's invisible presence, always within and among us. The church continues Christ's work in the world.

Living Faith: A Statement of Christian Belief was published by our denomination in 1984 and accepted as a contemporary statement of our faith. This 37 page booklet is widely used in our churches for both teaching and worship.

MODE OF WORSHIP

Weekly Sunday worship services include prayers, hymns, scripture readings and a sermon, and sometimes the Lord's Supper (varying in frequency according to congregation from 4 times per year to monthly or even more regularly). We encourage personal prayer and Bible study.

STRUCTURE

The Presbyterian church is governed through a hierarchy of courts. These are not legal courts, but structures to regulate and guide church affairs. Congregations elect and ordain several members as elders. Along with the minister they form the court called the session to oversee the congregation's worship and pastoral care. (The minister is also called a teaching elder.) Congregations belong to regional presbyteries, which in turn compose synods. All congregations (through their elders) and ministers participate in these structures. All regional presbyteries are represented at an annual General Assembly which deals with questions of doctrine and government. The Assembly also provides direction on contemporary issues such as euthanasia and dealing with sexual abuse.

DIVISIONS/DENOMINATIONS

None. We accept a range of belief on many issues, and where serious differences exist, we follow specific procedures to resolve them pastorally.

RITUALS

The two sacraments we celebrate are the Lord's Supper and baptism of believers and believers' children. Another ritual performed is ordination, in which ministers and elders are set apart for their specific function in the church. Individuals and congregations may have other meaningful rituals such as commissioning of teachers in the congregation, laying on of hands during prayer, etc..

LAWS

As Jesus said,

> You shall love the Lord your God with all your heart, and with all your soul, and with all your mind. This is the greatest and first commandment. And a second is like it: You shall love your neighbour as yourself. On these two commandments hang all the law and the prophets. (Matthew 22:37-40)

These laws are foremost. Under them come the other biblical laws such as the Ten Commandments, as they are interpreted for our contemporary situations. There are also the church government laws, detailed in the section entitled *Structure*, above.

MODE OF DRESS/MODESTY REQUIREMENTS

Not Applicable

DIETARY REQUIREMENTS

None, although some Presbyterians regard drinking of alcoholic beverages as sinful.

HOLY DAYS/FESTIVALS

Every Sunday is a festival for worship and rest. Christmas (celebrating Jesus Christ's birth), Good Friday and Easter (Jesus Christ's death and resurrection) are the most important festivals. In recent years more congregations have celebrated the entire church year including Advent, Epiphany, Lent and Pentecost.

BELIEFS AND PRACTICES REGARDING DEATH

BELIEFS

The following passage from *Living Faith* (please see reference in the section entitled *Basic Beliefs*) expresses our beliefs about death in the context of our trust in God's love and power, which we understand only in part:

> We shall all stand under the final judgment of God,
> as we receive the divine verdict on our lives.
> Worthy of hell, eternal separation from God,

our hope is for heaven, eternal life with God
through the grace bestowed on us in Christ.
To say "no" to Christ is to refuse life
and to embrace death.
The destiny of all people
is in the hands of God
whose mercy and justice we trust.

Eternal life is resurrection life.
As God raised Christ,
so shall we be raised
into a condition fit for life with God.
Eternal life begins in this life:
whoever believes in the Son of God
already has eternal life.
In Baptism by faith we die and rise with Christ
and so are one with the risen Lord.
In death we commit our future confidently to God.
(*Living Faith*, 10:3-10:4)

PRACTICES

As is the cultural norm, we embalm the deceased. A few days later mourners, family and friends gather for a funeral, a worship service led by a minister. The funeral is held either in the family's church or the funeral parlour. Both burial and cremation are accepted.

SPECIAL RELIGIOUS RITUALS WHICH CAN BE PERFORMED ONLY BY AN AUTHORIZED REPRESENTATIVE OF THIS FAITH

Only ordained ministers of word and sacraments may lead the sacrament of the Lord's Supper and, under normal circumstances, baptize. Ordained ministers of other Christian denominations also validly perform these sacraments. In emergency situations, non-ordained Christians may baptize.

SACRED WRITINGS REQUIRED

The Holy Bible, as detailed in the section entitled *Scriptures,* is our only sacred writing. Other devotional books and hymn books have spiritual value, but the Bible holds unique authority.

SACRED OBJECTS REQUIRED

None

SYMBOLS

The cross of Jesus Christ is our central symbol. The burning bush, through which God called Moses to his role in leading the Israelites from Egypt (Exodus 3-5) is a symbol which Presbyterians have chosen as our emblem, signifying the Lord's presence and call. We also value a wide variety of other biblical and Christian symbols as means of God's grace, such as the dove, the fish, bread and wine, the star and the grapevine.

This chapter was written by:
Rev. Fairlie Ritchie
for Ministry and Church Vocations
The Presbyterian Church in Canada
50 Wynford Drive
North York, Ontario
M3C 1J7
(416) 441-1111
Fax: (416) 441-2825

THE REFORMED CHURCH IN CANADA

FOUNDER

Historically speaking, many of the founding members of the Reformed Church in Canada were of Dutch origin. Although the Church has no founder as such, it recognizes the fact that various men and women have made their input upon the denomination's faith and practices.

NATURE OF RELIGION

Monotheistic; the Church believes in one God who makes Himself known as God the Father, God the Son and God the Holy Spirit.

SCRIPTURES

Both the Old and the New Testament books of the Bible are understood as the Word of God and are used for preaching, teaching and personal edification. There is no authorized translation but many prefer the Revised Standard Version or the New International Version.

BASIC BELIEFS

Some of the Reformed Church's basic beliefs are:

- God created the universe, the world, and humankind.
- "Sin" entered into the world. Sin manifests itself as disobedience or separation - separation from God, separation from one another, separation from creation and at times, separation from oneself.

The Reformed Church believes that God has not forsaken His creation but that He reaches out to it in love. The greatest manifestation of this love occurred when He sent His only son, Jesus Christ, into the world to bring about a reconciliation between God and His people. Believers in and followers of Jesus Christ are called Christians.

The Holy Bible is seen as the Book that teaches of God's love for and interactions with His people. The supreme example of this love is Christ's death on the Cross.

The three things every believer ought to know are:

- How great are one's sins and miseries.
- How, with God's help, one may be set free from these sins and miseries.
- How one can learn to express gratitude to God for such deliverance.

MODE OF WORSHIP

Believers usually attend Sunday worship services, and are encouraged to spend time in private prayer and bible reading at home.

STRUCTURE

The Reformed Church in Canada is an integral part of the Reformed Church in America. As such it is part of one of the oldest Protestant denominations in North America.

The Reformed Church believes that all Christians are called to the ministry of believers. Lay people may be called and ordained as Elders and/or Deacons. Pastors, Elders and Deacons in each local parish make up the governing body within that parish.

DIVISIONS/DENOMINATIONS

The Reformed Church in Canada is part of the Reformed family of denominations that have their origin in the Protestant Reformation of the sixteenth century.

RITUALS

Baptism: The Church practices infant and believers' baptism. It believes that children of believing parents are included in God's covenant with His people and are invited to accept the sign of the covenant, baptism. Baptism is also seen as an initiation into the Body of Christ, the Church.

Holy Communion: The Sacrament of Holy Communion (the Lord's Supper), is sacred in the life of the Church. It is administered at least four times a year but preferably more frequently.

Ordination: Through ordination, the congregation sets a person aside for a special function within the body of believers. Ordination is open to both men and women.

Both the sacraments of Baptism and Holy Communion should be administered within the context of the Church's ministry, that is within the worshipping community. Ordained clergy preach God's Word and administer the Sacraments, although lay persons may be given permission to perform these tasks.

In addition to preaching and instructing the Word and administering the Sacraments, a high priority is given in the Reformed Church to visiting the sick and needy.

LAWS

The Reformed Church seeks to adhere to the guiding principles set forth in the Ten Commandments (the Law), and in the Summary of the Law (Matthew 22:37-40).

MODE OF DRESS/MODESTY REQUIREMENTS

Not Applicable

DIETARY REQUIREMENTS

There is no special diet for members of the Reformed Church, although they are urged to respect their bodies and see them as Temples of the Holy Spirit.

HOLY DAYS/FESTIVALS

The Reformed Church in Canada follows the general holy days of the Christian calendar.

BELIEFS AND PRACTICES REGARDING DEATH

BELIEFS

- In the time of death, the church witnesses to its faith in a life eternal.
- Most families prefer burial, although some choose cremation.

PRACTICES

- Families and friends are encouraged to call their pastor when death occurs in order that he or she may provide support to the family.
- Families are encouraged to hold funeral services at the place where the Christian family gathers for worship.

SPECIAL RELIGIOUS RITUALS WHICH CAN BE PERFORMED ONLY BY AN AUTHORIZED REPRESENTATIVE OF THIS FAITH

Generally, an ordained pastor preaches the Word and administers the sacraments. However, when a special need arises the Board of Elders may give permission to an Elder to perform these functions.

SACRED WRITINGS REQUIRED

The Holy Bible.

SACRED OBJECTS REQUIRED

None

SYMBOLS

The symbols used at worship are an open Bible, a baptismal font and a communion table with the communion cup. Various symbols of the cross are also used at worship.

RELIGIOUS NEEDS

Individuals in institutions are encouraged to inform the local congregation/pastor, so that the community may provide visits, prayer and spiritual support.

This chapter was written by:
Rev. Will Kroon
Reformed Church in Canada
c/o West Park Hospital
82 Buttonwood Avenue
Toronto, Ontario
M6M 2J5
(416) 243-3600 ext. 2401

Other Contact:
Council of the Reformed Church in Canada
R.R. 4
Cambridge, Ontario
N1R 5S5

THE ROMAN CATHOLIC CHURCH

FOUNDER

The Roman Catholic Church was founded by Jesus Christ almost two thousand years ago.

NATURE OF RELIGION

The Roman Catholic faith is monotheistic and trinitarian. The Church teaches that God, who is one, has revealed himself to humanity as a Trinity of Persons - the Father, the Son and the Holy Spirit.

SCRIPTURES AND RELIGIOUS BOOKS

The authorized translations of the bible used by Roman Catholics include the New Jerusalem, New American and New Revised Standard Version (Catholic edition). Other religious books include lectionaries and sacramentaries used in the celebration of Mass (also called the Eucharist), Sunday and daily missals for general use, the Roman Ritual (now ordinarily divided into separate liturgical books for the celebration of each sacrament) and hymnals (e.g. *Catholic Book of Worship, Glory and Praise*). Books and booklets of traditional and modern prayers for private use are available in a variety of forms.[1]

BASIC BELIEFS

The general overview of the Christian faith outlined in this edition of the Multifaith Information Manual under the title *Christianity* includes the majority of the Roman Catholic Church's basic beliefs.

The essential elements of the Roman Catholic faith have been summarized and synthesized in the form of *professions of faith* or *creeds* (from Latin *credo:* "I believe"). Among these, the *Apostles' Creed* and the *Nicene Creed* occupy a special place.

A much fuller expression of Roman Catholic beliefs and practices has been recently published in the universal *Catechism of the Catholic Church.*[2]

MODE OF WORSHIP

The central expression of worship for Roman Catholics is the celebration of the Eucharist, described as the "source and summit of the Christian life". The Catholic theology of the Eucharist can be summarized in these words: "At the Last Supper, on the night he was betrayed, our Saviour instituted the Eucharistic sacrifice of his Body and Blood. This he did in order to perpetuate the sacrifice of the cross throughout the ages until he should come again, and so to entrust to his beloved Spouse, the Church, a memorial of his death and resurrection: a sacrament of love, a sign of unity, a bond of charity, a Paschal banquet in which Christ is consumed, the mind is filled with grace, and a pledge of future glory is given to us."[3]

The celebration of the seven sacraments (please refer to the section entitled *Rituals,* below) involves the action of Christ and the Church in communicating, through ritual and symbol, the fruits of Christ's life, death and resurrection to his people. There are also other devotions, though of lesser importance, through which Roman Catholic believers participate in the praise and worship of God, in meditation and in communal intercession for the needs of the Church and world.

There are Catholics of the Eastern rite in union with Rome (please refer to the section entitled *Structure*, below) who retain their own liturgies (public worship) and customs.

STRUCTURE

The Roman Catholic Church is characterized by a hierarchic structure of bishops and priests in which doctrinal and disciplinary authority are dependent upon apostolic succession (i.e. from the twelve apostles), with the pope as the head of the college of bishops.

The Roman Catholic Church in Canada comprises 74 dioceses, of which 65 are of the Latin rite, 8 of the Eastern rite (i.e. Ukrainian, Melkite, Maronite and Slovak eparchies) and one military ordinariate. There are 16 dioceses in the Province of Ontario. Each diocese is a unit of the world-wide Church, of which the Pope, the Bishop of Rome, is the visible head. Dioceses are under the direction of bishops who, as members of the college of bishops, are one with the Pope in responsibility for the guidance and direction of the Church. The bishops of Canada are united, for practical and pastoral reasons, in a national conference (the Canadian Conference of Catholic Bishops) and regional conferences (in this province, the Ontario Conference of Catholic Bishops).

Within each diocese is the parish structure, with parishioners and pastor (parish priest) forming a community around the parish church. The pastor, appointed by, accountable to, and in collaboration with the local bishop, has pastoral responsibility for Roman Catholics within the boundaries of his parish.

The Church also features communities of women or men religious, under their own superiors, dedicated to the spiritual and pastoral needs of all. They collaborate closely in diocesan ministry and pastoral activities and are often assigned parochial (parish) as well as non-parochial roles in a diocese.

DIVISIONS/DENOMINATIONS

Not applicable.

RITUALS

As mentioned above in the section entitled *Mode of Worship*, the Roman Catholic Church recognizes seven sacraments instituted by Christ: Baptism, Confirmation, the Eucharist, Penance (Reconciliation), the Anointing of the Sick, Holy Orders and Matrimony. Communion of the Sick is the rite in which the previously consecrated Eucharist is brought to the ill and infirm. The Eucharist as viaticum ("food for the journey") is administered to the dying. These are the most significant, though not the only, religious rituals of the Church.

Catholics of the Eastern rite in union with Rome (please refer to the section entitled *Structure*, above) celebrate their own religious rituals and customs.

LAWS

Laws and precepts in their various forms are seen by the Roman Catholic Church as essential to good order in society, and in individuals' and communities' lives. The Church teaches that the moral law contains within it the natural law, the Old Law (especially the Ten Commandments), and the New Law (or the Law of the Gospel).

The Code of Canon Law (1983) is the Roman Catholic Church's fundamental legislative document, based on the juridical and legislative heritage of revelation and tradition.[4] In addition, there are the "Precepts of the Church", which delineate basic obligations of Roman Catholics in such matters as attendance at Mass on Sundays and holy days, the reception of the sacraments of Penance and the Eucharist, and the observation of the prescribed days of fasting and abstinence.

MODE OF DRESS/MODESTY REQUIREMENTS

There is no particular code of dress for Roman Catholics. Modesty in clothing is mandated as an important element in the recognition and preservation of the dignity and holiness of persons.

DIETARY REQUIREMENTS

There are no specific dietary requirements for Roman Catholics. All are encouraged to practice moderation in the consumption of food and drink, and to practice forms of penance, including fasting and abstinence (from meat), in keeping with age, health and other considerations.

Christian fasting obtains its full meaning when Christians deprive themselves of food in order to be more open to prayer, to share more in the suffering of those who are starving, and to save money to give to the poor. Fasting among Christians is a penitential discipline intended to open their hearts to God and others, a means of purification and spiritual liberation, and a witness of the believer's depth of faith.

Abstinence from meat on Fridays throughout the year is a traditional value of Roman Catholics, observed as a form of penance in memory of the Lord's death on Good Friday. Catholics may substitute special acts of charity or piety on this day.[5]

The seasons and days of penance in the course of the Church year (Lent and each Friday) are intense moments of the Church's penitential practice. Ash Wednesday and Good Friday are designated as days of fasting and abstinence.

HOLY DAYS/FESTIVALS

The Sunday celebration of the Lord's Day and the Eucharist is at the heart of Catholic life. Each Sunday is celebrated as the day of Christ's Resurrection. The celebration of the Easter

Triduum (Holy Thursday, Good Friday, Holy Saturday, Easter Sunday) is central to the Church year. There are also other feasts, called *holy days*, which celebrate various aspects of the mystery of salvation in Christ. These holy days include the feast of Mary, the Mother of God (January 1), and Christmas.

Roman Catholics have an obligation to participate in the Mass on Sundays and holy days of obligation. They are also to refrain from engaging in work or activities that hinder the worship owed to God, the joy proper to the Lord's Day, the performance of the works of mercy, and the appropriate relaxation of mind and body. It is recognized that family needs or important social service can legitimately excuse Catholics from the obligation of Sunday rest.[6]

BELIEFS AND PRACTICES REGARDING DEATH

BELIEFS

The Church teaches that death entered the world as a consequence of sin. Jesus Christ, through his own death and resurrection, has transformed the curse of death into a blessing. Because of him, Christian death holds a positive meaning.[7]

The Roman Catholic perspective on death can be summarized thus: it is the end of the earthly pilgrimage, of the time of God's grace and mercy, offered so that people may work out their earthly life in keeping with the divine plan, and decide their ultimate destiny.[8] This "ultimate destiny" is either heaven or hell.

Since it is "appointed for mortals to die once, and after that the judgment",[9] the Catholic faith rejects belief in reincarnation.

Belief in eternal life and the resurrection of the body are the foundations of hope in the face of death. The Church encourages its members to prepare for the hour of death, and assists in that preparation in a particular way through the sacraments of Penance (Reconciliation), the Anointing of the Sick and the Eucharist as viaticum. Death can then be faced with renewed or deepened confidence in the presence and power of the Risen Lord, the source of life and salvation.

The Church teaches that dying persons should be given particular attention and care to help them live their last days and hours in dignity and peace. Such attention and care is directed toward the spiritual, physical, emotional and mental well-being of the dying person and his or her family and friends. The loving attentiveness and faith-filled prayer of the individual's family and friends, so vital in itself, is enhanced and strengthened by the pastoral (spiritual and religious) care offered by the community of the Church.

PRACTICES

Pastoral care, including sacramental care, is central in assisting the dying person's preparation to leave this earthly life and meet the Lord. The presence of the Roman Catholic priest (especially for the celebration of the sacraments of Penance and the Anointing of the Sick), and the pastoral care offered by the deacon, men and women religious and the lay faithful is important to Roman Catholics as they begin to approach death. The celebration of the sacrament of Penance liberates the person from sin and guilt and enables him or her to experience the Lord's healing gift of mercy and salvation. The Sacrament of Anointing of the Sick, given to those who suffer from serious illness and infirmity, is especially important for those at the point of departing from this life.[10]

The Church also offers the Eucharist as viaticum to those about to die. The sacrament of Christ dead and now risen, the Eucharist becomes the sacrament of passing from death to life, from this world to the Father.[11] There are also prayers in the Church's ritual to be offered prior to, at the time of, and after death for the needs of the dying or deceased person and his or her family.

The bodies of the dead are to be treated with respect and charity, in faith and hope of the resurrection. The burial of the dead is a corporal work of mercy which honours the children of God, who are temples of the Holy Spirit.[12]

The Funeral Mass, celebrated in the parish church, is the usual funeral rite, whereas funeral prayers and committal service without Mass is the exception rather than the rule.

Autopsies can be morally permitted for legal inquests or scientific research. The free gift of organs after death is legitimate and can be meritorious. The Church permits cremation, provided that it does not demonstrate a denial of faith in the resurrection of the body.[13]

SPECIAL RELIGIOUS RITUALS WHICH CAN BE PERFORMED ONLY BY AN AUTHORIZED REPRESENTATIVE OF THIS FAITH

For Roman Catholics, there are specific needs in the area of worship and the sacraments that can be fulfilled only by those ordained or mandated by their Church through the office and ministry of the bishop.

There are three orders of ordained ministry in the Roman Catholic Church: bishop, priest and deacon. Bishops alone ordain and are the ordinary ministers of Confirmation. Priests share with bishops the responsibility and privilege of celebrating the Eucharist, granting absolution in the sacrament of Penance and administering the sacrament of Anointing of the

Sick. The ordinary minister of Baptism is a priest or deacon, although in a life-threatening situation anyone, including a person who is not a Roman Catholic, can validly baptize. Bishops, priests and deacons ordinarily officiate at the sacrament of Matrimony. They also exercise the ministry of teaching and preaching.

Deacons and women and men religious are involved in many forms of ministry, including pastoral care ministry in parishes and institutions. The growing number of trained and mandated (by the bishop) lay faithful has brought increased vitality to pastoral care ministry within the Church. In addition to offering their many personal and pastoral gifts in service to the Church and its ministry to those in need, the lay faithful may also be mandated by the bishop and pastor as ministers of the Eucharist. They are then in a position to bring the Eucharist to the ill, aged and infirm in the parish, and to those in institutional settings.

There is no intercommunion (ie. no shared sacraments, including the Eucharist), between the Roman Catholic Church and other denominations and faith groups. It is therefore especially important that Roman Catholics within provincial institutions have the opportunity to participate in the Eucharist and to receive the sacraments on a regular basis from qualified and mandated representatives of their Church.

This implies in a special way the ministry of priests, particularly in the celebration of the Eucharist and the sacraments of Penance and Anointing of the Sick. It implies also the sacramental ministry of deacons, men and women religious, and mandated lay faithful.

The theological, moral and spiritual underpinnings of pastoral counselling and spiritual guidance of Roman Catholics are sufficiently distinct from those of other denominations and faith groups as to necessitate access to counselling and spiritual guidance from a qualified, mandated representative of the Roman Catholic Church.

SACRED WRITINGS REQUIRED

Please refer to the above section entitled *Scriptures*.

SACRED OBJECTS REQUIRED

Many Roman Catholics wish to have the use of a bible, blessed crucifix, rosary, medals, icons/holy pictures and other religious books and articles to enhance their meditation and prayer life.

SYMBOLS

In Church art, symbols arose as early as the third century and were used to represent persons and mysteries. The central Christian symbol is the cross. For Catholics, the cross also takes the form of the crucifix, on which there is a representation of the crucified Christ.

ECUMENISM AND INTERFAITH DIALOGUE

The Roman Catholic Church engages in active ecumenical and interfaith exchanges and dialogue, always according to the directives of the pope and bishops. The Church is sensitive to the rights of persons of all denominations and faith groups to have access to, and to receive, spiritual and religious care in a manner appropriate to the beliefs and practices of their denominations and faith groups.

ENDNOTES

[1]   One of the most popular and affordable booklets (less than $1.00) is the 24-page *Everyday Catholic Prayers*. The accompanying *Handbook for Today's Catholic: Beliefs, Practices, Prayers* (65 pages, $2.00) is another helpful resource. (Liguori Publications, One Liguori Dr., Liguori, Missouri 63057-9999)

[2]   *Catechism of the Catholic Church* (Published in Canada by Publications Service, Canadian Conference of Catholic Bishops, 90 Parent Ave., Ottawa, Ontario K1N 7B1, 1994, 698 pages)

[3]   Ibid, # 1323

[4]   *Code of Canon Law* (Publications Service, Canadian Conference of Catholic Bishops, 90 Parent Ave., Ottawa, Ontario K1N 7B1, 1994), p. xiii

[5]   *Guidelines for Pastoral Liturgy, Liturgical Calendar, 1993-94* (Canadian Conference of Catholic Bishops, 90 Parent Ave., Ottawa, Ontario K1N 7B1), pp 55-6

[6]   *Catechism of the Catholic Church*, cf. #s 2180 & 2185

[7]   Ibid, cf. # 1009-10

[8]   Ibid, cf. # 1013

[9]   *Letter to the Hebrews*, chapter 9, verse 27 (NRSV)

[10] *Catechism of the Catholic Church*, cf. # 1523

[11] Ibid, cf. # 1524

[12] Ibid, cf. # 2300

[13] Ibid, cf. # 2301

This chapter was written by:
Fr. Brian McNally
OMCSRC Representative
Ontario Conference of Catholic Bishops   (613) 283-0220
St. Francis de Sales Rectory
17 Elmsley Street North, Box 1153
Smiths Falls, Ontario
K7A 5B4

THE SALVATION ARMY

FOUNDER

Founded in London, England by the Reverend William Booth in 1865, The Salvation Army was originally known as The Christian Mission. Today it is an internationally active and respected religious and charitable organization operating in 100 countries.

William Booth began preaching in the Methodist Church while still in his early twenties. However, he felt a deep-seated conviction to minister to the masses who were trapped in the depressing social conditions of Victorian England. His wife Catherine shared this conviction, which led them to commence tent meetings in a disused Quaker graveyard in London's east end. It was there among the drunks, prostitutes, gamblers and thieves that Booth found his destiny.

By 1885, the Salvation Army had grown to 250,000 members. The evangelical zeal of the converts and immigrants carried the Salvation Army's message to virtually every country in the world.

The Salvation Army came to Canada in 1882 when 2 English immigrant lay Salvationists began holding outdoor services in London, Ontario. Operations quickly expanded eastward to Newfoundland in 1886, westward to British Columbia in 1887, and northward to the Yukon and Northwest Territories in 1898.

NATURE OF RELIGION

Monotheistic; the Salvation Army, as an international movement, is an evangelical branch of the Christian Church.

Its message is based upon the Bible; its ministry is motivated by love for God and a practical concern for humanity's needs.

Its mission is to preach the Gospel of Jesus Christ, supply basic human needs, provide personal counselling, and undertake the spiritual and moral regeneration and physical rehabilitation of all persons in need who come within its sphere of influence regardless of race, colour, creed, sex or age.

SCRIPTURES

The Salvation Army's first tenet of faith states that the Scriptures of the Old and New Testaments were given by inspiration from God, and that they alone constitute the divine rule of Christian faith and practice.

BASIC BELIEFS

Salvationists believe:

- The Scriptures of the Old and New Testaments were given by inspiration from God, and they alone constitute the divine rule of Christian faith and practice.

- There is only one God who is infinitely perfect; the Creator, Preserver and Governor of all things, and who is the only proper object of religious worship.

- There are three persons in the Godhead; the Father, the Son and the Holy Ghost, undivided in essence and co-equal in power and glory.

- In the person of Jesus Christ, the Divine and human natures are united, so that He is truly and properly God and truly and properly man.

- Our first parents were created in a state of innocence, but by their disobedience they lost their purity and happiness. Consequently, all men and women have become sinners, totally depraved, and as such are justly exposed to God's wrath.

- The Lord Jesus Christ has by His suffering and death made an atonement for the whole world so that whosoever will follow Him may be saved.

- Repentance to God, faith in our Lord Jesus Christ, and regeneration by the Holy Spirit are necessary for salvation.

- We are justified by grace through faith in our Lord Jesus Christ, and those who believeth hath the witness in themselves.

- Continuance in a state of salvation depends upon continued obedient faith in Christ.

- It is the privilege of all believers to be wholly sanctified, that their whole spirit, soul and body will be preserved blameless unto the return of our Lord Jesus Christ.

- The soul is immortal; we also believe in the resurrection of the body; in the general judgement at the world's end; in the eternal happiness of the righteous; and in the endless punishment of the wicked.

MODE OF WORSHIP

The mode of worship varies but always includes a Bible centred address with the opportunity for personal response by those present. A unique feature of the Army's religious expression is its joyful instrumental, vocal and congregational music. Music symbolizes the Salvationist's cheerful religion and also serves as a form of creative recreation.

The brass band is the most traditional form of Salvation Army music. However, the Salvationist's exuberant faith also expresses itself through songster brigades, string bands and various combos.

In addition to the Army's traditional street meetings, we also hold Sunday schools and public morning and evening worship services each Sunday at every Salvation Army Corps (Church).

STRUCTURE

A quasi-military command structure was formed in 1878 when the title "The Salvation Army" was adopted. A similarly practical organization today enables resources to be equally flexible.

Evangelistic and social enterprises are maintained under the General's authority by full time officers and employees, as well as by soldiers who give service in their free time.

DIVISIONS/DENOMINATIONS

The Salvation Army, a worldwide movement working in 100 countries, is a Protestant denomination within the evangelical, Christian tradition. It has been rightly described as "an evangelical church with an acute social conscience".

There are 5 Divisional Headquarters in Ontario. These are located in the following cities:

- Ontario East Division, located in Kingston.
- Ontario Metro Toronto Division, located in Scarborough.
- Ontario North Division, located in Orillia.
- Ontario South Division, located in Hamilton.
- Ontario West Division, located in London.

RITUALS

From its beginnings, The Salvation Army has adopted a non-sacramental stance. However, children are dedicated at an early age and there are two levels of soldiership (membership), junior from 7 to 14 years of age and senior from 14 and up. Preceding enrollment as a soldier, a profession of salvation by faith is given. The Salvation Army also follows the Armenian and Wesleyan tradition of Holiness teaching and theology. Marriages and funerals are important ceremonies and rites of passage.

LAWS

Not Applicable

MODE OF DRESS/MODESTY REQUIREMENTS

Officers are required to wear the uniform of their rank for all official Salvation Army activities. Many Salvation Army soldiers also choose to wear the official uniform as a witness to their faith and an opportunity to render service through our many social and community programs.

All Salvation Army soldiers are encouraged to dress modestly when not in uniform.

DIETARY REQUIREMENTS

Salvationists pledge to abstain from the use of alcohol or tobacco in any form. They also promise to abstain from any non-prescription drugs. There are no other forbidden foods.

HOLY DAYS/FESTIVALS

As part of the Christian church, Salvationists follow the general Holy days of the Christian calendar.

BELIEFS AND PRACTICES REGARDING DEATH

BELIEFS

As our doctrine sets forth, Salvationists believe "in the immortality of the soul; in the resurrection of the body; in the general judgement at the world's end; in the eternal happiness of the righteous; and in the endless punishment of the wicked."

PRACTICES

Salvationists consider the person who "dies in the Lord" to be promoted to glory. Although there is sadness at the loss, there is joy in the departed's "home going". The funeral service is a time of celebration and a reaffirmation of faith in God's promise of eternal life.

SPECIAL RELIGIOUS RITUALS WHICH CAN BE PERFORMED ONLY BY AN AUTHORIZED REPRESENTATIVE OF THIS FAITH

A commissioned officer must perform child dedications, marriages and funerals.

SACRED WRITINGS REQUIRED

The Salvation Army uses many translations of the Bible, the most common being the New International Version. The *Salvation Army Song Book* is used for worship services and personal devotions.

SACRED OBJECTS REQUIRED

None

SYMBOLS

The Flag: Designed by Catherine Booth, the flag was introduced in 1878. The central yellow star, or sun, represents the Holy Spirit's fire, the third person in the Trinity. The red background represents the blood of Jesus Christ; and the surrounding blue border, the purity of God.

The Crest: Designed by Captain William H. Ebdon in 1878, the crest graphically illustrates the Army's fundamental doctrines. The cross with its entwined "S" speaks of Salvation through the Lord Jesus Christ. Crossed swords imply a determination to fight against sin and social injustice, guided by the gospel's truth. This is surrounded by the sun which represents the fire and light of the Holy Spirit. The words "Blood and Fire" refer to Jesus Christ's shed blood and the refining fire of the Holy Spirit. The crown symbolizes the eternal reward of the faithful Christian soldier.

The Salute: Raising the right hand above the shoulder with the index finger pointing upward is used to recognize and greet fellow citizens and travelers to the heavenly Kingdom.

SCHOOLS AND INSTITUTIONS

There are 2 Colleges for Officer Training in Canada. One is located in Toronto, Ontario and the other is in St. John's, Newfoundland. All officers (clergy) for the territory are trained at one of these schools.

The Catherine Booth Bible College located in Winnipeg, Manitoba offers several degrees and prepares lay salvationists for ministry.

SOCIAL SERVICE AND COMMUNITY INVOLVEMENT

The Salvation Army is the largest social service provider other than the government itself. These services include:

- Residential facilities for women and children.
- Courtroom counselling
- Prison visits and interviews.
- Chaplaincy services
- Parole and probation supervision.
- Residential Hostels
- Halfway Houses
- Addictions rehabilitation services.
- Detox and mental health units.
- General hospitals
- Personal care senior citizen homes
- Visitation to the lonely and shut-ins.
- Summer camps
- Youth programs
- Family Services
- Emergency Disaster Services
- Family Tracing Service

This chapter was written by:
Major Ronald J. Bowles
Assistant Public Relations Secretary
Communications and Special Events
The Salvation Army, Canada and Bermuda
(416) 340-2162
20 Salvation Square,
Toronto, Ontario
M5G 2H3

Mailing address:
P.O. Box 4021, Postal Station A
Toronto, Ontario
M5W 2B1

THE SEVENTH-DAY ADVENTIST CHURCH

FOUNDER

Not Provided

NATURE OF RELIGION

Monotheistic, Christian

SCRIPTURES

- The Bible is the sole rule of faith and practice.

- The inspirational writings of Ellen G. White are an aid to Bible interpretation.

BASIC BELIEFS

(For a detailed description of beliefs, please refer to the overview entitled *Christianity*, at the beginning of the Christian portion of this manual.)

- There is one God, the Father, Son and Holy Spirit, a unity of three co-eternal Persons commonly called the Trinity. God the father is the Creator, Source, Sustainer and Sovereign of all creation. God the eternal Son became incarnate in Jesus Christ, revealing the character of God and through whom humanity's salvation is accomplished. God the Holy Spirit draws men and women to Himself and extends spiritual gifts to the Church.

- The second coming of Christ is the grand climax of the gospel. His coming will be literal, personal, visible and world-wide. When He returns the righteous dead will be resurrected and together with the righteous living will be glorified and taken to heaven for 1000 years. A second resurrection will take place after this time for the unrighteous, who will be destroyed by a cleansing fire of this earth, while a new earth will be established for the righteous to inhabit eternally.

- Death is a state of temporary unconsciousness, awaiting the resurrection at Christ's return.

MODE OF WORSHIP

Not Provided

STRUCTURE

- The Seventh-Day Adventist Church is led by ordained ministers.
- The Church uses a representative system.

DIVISIONS/DENOMINATIONS

Not Provided

RITUALS

- Baptism is performed by water immersion.
- Holy Communion is celebrated quarterly.

LAWS

Not Provided

MODE OF DRESS/MODESTY REQUIREMENTS

Not Provided

DIETARY REQUIREMENTS

In order to enjoy maximum emotional and physical wellness, 8 principles are encouraged:

- Nutritious Food; a balanced vegetarian diet provides the healthiest lifestyle. Only flesh foods identified as "clean" in scripture may be consumed.

- Drug-Free Living; members are encouraged to lead a drug-free life. Members abstain from alcoholic beverages, tobacco, and other drugs and narcotics including milder gateway drugs found in tea, coffee and colas.

- Exercise

- Fresh air

- Sunlight

- Water

- Rest

- Trust

Exercise and fresh air offer natural stimulation. Sunlight, water, rest, and trust in divine power are soothing relaxants.

HOLY DAYS/FESTIVALS

The Sabbath: The Creator rested on the seventh day and instituted the Sabbath as a memorial of Creation. It is a day of communion with God and one another.

Observance: All members cease from work on the Sabbath. Activities that enhance communication with God are proper; those which distract from that purpose and turn the Sabbath into a holiday are improper. The day begins at sunset on Friday evening and ends at sunset Saturday evening.

BELIEFS AND PRACTICES REGARDING DEATH

Not Provided

SPECIAL RELIGIOUS RITUALS WHICH CAN BE PERFORMED ONLY BY AN AUTHORIZED REPRESENTATIVE OF THIS FAITH

Not Provided

SACRED WRITINGS REQUIRED

Not Provided

SACRED OBJECTS REQUIRED

Not Provided

SYMBOLS

Not Provided

RESOURCES

- Local district pastors.

- Directors at Ontario Conference Headquarters.

- Prison Ministries;

- Rev. Clarence Baptiste, OMCSRC Representative
  34 Henry Welsh Dr.
  Willowdale, Ontario M2R 3P4
  (416) 663-0887

THE UNITED CHURCH OF CANADA

FOUNDER

The United Church of Canada, as one expression of the Christian religion, was founded by Jesus Christ. The United Church is a distinct Canadian Church which came into being on June 10, 1925 through an Act of Parliament at the request of the uniting churches; the Methodist Church, the Congregational Churches of Canada and the Presbyterian Church in Canada. One third of the Presbyterian congregations chose not to enter the Union. A subsequent union between the United Church and the Canada Conference of the Evangelical United Brethren Church was inaugurated on January 10, 1968.

NATURE OF RELIGION

Monotheistic, Christian; the worship of God in the mystery of the Holy Trinity; Creator, Son and Holy Spirit.

SCRIPTURES

The sacred scriptures are those of the Hebrew tradition known as the Old Testament, and the New Testament.

BASIC BELIEFS

- God's holiness, mercy and justice.

- God's revelation in history, nature and supremely in Jesus Christ.

- God is the Creator, and created humankind in God's own image.

- Humans are prone to sin.

- Jesus Christ is the only mediator between God and humankind.

- Jesus was crucified, died and rose from the dead.

- Jesus is the church's foundation, whereby followers gather for worship which consists of scripture reading, prayer and praise.

- There is life after death.

MODE OF WORSHIP

Congregations of believers gather weekly to worship God. A Service Book provides the Order of Service with latitude for varying forms of worship.

STRUCTURE

Church government is conciliar and exists on four levels:

- The local congregation.

- The Presbytery, consisting of from 10-40 congregations.

- The Conference, consisting of from 5-15 Presbyteries.

- The General Council, the national body which makes decisions on church polity, practice and programs. Each court of the church consists of equal numbers of clergy and laity.

DIVISIONS/DENOMINATIONS

The United Church of Canada is of the Reformed tradition of Protestantism. At Baptism those baptized are declared to be "received into the holy catholic church".

RITUALS

We observe the two sacraments of the Christian Church; Baptism (both infant and adult) and Holy Communion. The latter is observed weekly, monthly or quarterly as each congregation may decide. The recital of *A New Creed* authorized by The General Council in 1968 accompanies these observances.

LAWS

Few laws exist with regard to personal belief and practice, but strong models of personal faith, morals, integrity and personal responsibility are upheld.

MODE OF DRESS/MODESTY REQUIREMENTS

No single mandatory mode of dress is laid down for clergy or laity. Practices vary widely concerning wearing clergical garb to conduct public worship services.

DIETARY REQUIREMENTS

None

HOLY DAYS/FESTIVALS

Christmas: The celebration of Christ's birth.

Easter: The celebration of Christ's death and resurrection.

Pentecost: The celebration of the gift of the Holy Spirit and the birth of the Christian Church.

BELIEFS AND PRACTICES REGARDING DEATH

BELIEFS

The Church believes that death is a part of life, and that grief is a natural experience in the loss of a loved one. Hope around death is based upon the belief of life after death.

PRACTICES

A believer's remains are cremated or buried with dignity and respect, accompanied by a ritual service celebrating the deceased's life and commending his or her soul to a compassionate and merciful God.

SPECIAL RELIGIOUS RITUALS WHICH CAN BE PERFORMED ONLY BY AN AUTHORIZED REPRESENTATIVE OF THIS FAITH

Only those persons authorized by the church through ordination may conduct the sacraments of Baptism and Holy Communion, and officiate at the ordinance of Marriage. Exceptions are made under special circumstances.

SACRED WRITINGS REQUIRED

The sacred writings are those known as the Old and New Testaments, commonly called the Holy Bible. The Bible is used for personal devotion, public worship and comfort in times of bereavement.

SACRED OBJECTS REQUIRED

The Cross is uniformly found in all churches. The elements of bread and wine are used in the sacrament of Holy Communion.

SYMBOLS

Not Applicable.

SCHOOLS AND INSTITUTIONS

The United Church of Canada maintains the following schools:

- 11 Theological Colleges
- 6 Post Secondary Schools
- 3 Secondary Schools

SERVICE TO OTHERS

The United Church, since its inception, has placed strong emphasis on social action. Throughout its history the church has taken up social, ethical and moral issues with governing bodies at both community and national levels. Words became action as the church first established homes for unmarried mothers, homes for senior citizens and low cost housing for the poor. Coalition with other faith groups resulted in statements and programs on matters of justice, peace and ecology.

This chapter was written by:
Rev. Arch McCurdy
United Church Representative
Ontario Multifaith Council on Spiritual and Religious Care

For more Information, contact:
The General Council Office
The United Church of Canada
85 St. Clair Avenue East
Toronto, Ontario
M4T 1M8
(416) 925-4850

New Address after April 1, 1995:
3250 Bloor Street West
Toronto, Ontario

THE WORLDWIDE CHURCH OF GOD

FOUNDER

The Worldwide Church of God, originally the Radio Church of God, was established in Eugene, Oregon in 1933 through the evangelistic efforts of Herbert W. Armstrong. It took its present name in 1968.

As a result of the radio ministry's work, congregations were established throughout North America, and beginning in 1953, the rest of the world. Mr. Armstrong also established the World Tomorrow program, the Plain Truth magazine, Ambassador College and Ambassador Foundation. He served as pastor general of the Worldwide Church of God until his death in 1986.[1]

NATURE OF RELIGION

Monotheistic, Christian

SCRIPTURES

The Holy Scriptures comprise the canonical books of the Old and New Testaments. They are the inspired Word of God, the foundation of truth, and the accurate record of God's revelation to humanity. The Holy Scriptures constitute ultimate authority in all matters of doctrine and embody the infallible principles that govern all facets of Christian living (2 Timothy 3:15-17; 2 Peter 1:20-21; John 17:17).[2]

BASIC BELIEFS

- God, by the testimony of Scripture, is one divine Being in three eternal, co-essential, yet distinct hypostases or persons, Father, Son and Holy Spirit.

- Jesus is the Word, by whom and for whom God created all things. He is God, manifest in the flesh for our salvation.

- The Holy Spirit as the third hypostasis of the Godhead, the divine Comforter promised by Jesus Christ whom God sent to the Church on the Day of Pentecost.

- Salvation is deliverance from the bondage of sin and from the ultimate penalty of sin; death. Salvation is God's gift, given by grace through faith in Jesus Christ. It cannot be earned by personal merit or good works.

- Grace is the free, unmerited favour God bestows on a repentant sinner. By grace a person comes to know God, is justified and is saved.

- Repentance is a change of mind and attitude toward God, motivated by the Holy Spirit. Rather than a temporary, emotional response, repentance toward God results in an abiding change of thought, behaviour and life direction, in which a person resolutely turns to God, determines to forsake all sin and walk in all of God's commandments.

- The kingdom of God in the broadest sense is God's supreme sovereignty. God reigns both in the Church and in individual believers' lives once they submit to his will. God's kingdom will be established over the whole world after Jesus Christ's return and will increase, encompassing all things.

- In the Bible, the devil is named in many ways including Satan, adversary, evil one, murderer, liar, thief, tempter, accuser of the brethren, prince of demons and god of this world. He is in constant rebellion against God. His dominion and influence on humanity will cease at Jesus Christ's return.

- Christ's second coming will bring to an end the present age of human suffering and confusion.

- The millennium is the one thousand year period during which Jesus Christ and the resurrected saints rule the world in peace, justice and equity.

- Tithing is the scriptural practice of giving a tenth of one's increase to God.

- Racial prejudice and discrimination are unchristian. Jesus Christ taught that one of the great commandments is to love our neighbours as we love ourselves.

MODE OF WORSHIP

In addition to weekly Sabbath services and Bible studies, members are encouraged to conduct their lives with attitudes and behaviours consistent with Jesus Christ's teachings (John 4:24). Prayer and personal Bible study are the individual's responsibility.

STRUCTURE

The Worldwide Church of God maintains a hierarchical form of government. The Church's administration is led by the pastor general, who is supported by a board of directors and an advisory council of elders. Each congregation is led by a full-time pastor. Elders, deacons, deaconesses and lay members hold leadership roles under the pastor.[3]

Church Headquarters are located in Pasadena, California under which several Regional Offices operate around the world.

DIVISIONS/DENOMINATIONS

The Worldwide Church of God is a Protestant denomination of the Christian Church.

RITUALS

The Lord's Supper or New Testament Passover:	The annual partaking of bread and wine commemorating Christ's death for human sin. The service includes a footwashing ceremony.
Baptism:	Repentant believers are baptized by water immersion.
Fasting:	Members fast from sunset to sunset on the Day of Atonement.
Anointing the Sick:	The ministry provides laying on of hands to anoint the sick.
Ordination:	Laying on of hands is also used to ordain an individual to a position of service within the Church.

LAWS

Members are taught to adhere to Jesus Christ's example and teachings as the apostles and Gospel writers described in the New Testament. This includes keeping of the Ten Commandments

MODE OF DRESS/MODESTY REQUIREMENTS

The Church does not set strict standards by which people must dress, but asks that all members dress modestly and appropriately according to their means.

DIETARY REQUIREMENTS

The Church encourages its members to observe the biblical teaching concerning clean and unclean meats (Leviticus 11; and Deuteronomy 14).

HOLY DAYS/FESTIVALS

The observance of the festivals and holy days enjoined on ancient Israel was affirmed by the example of Jesus Christ and the apostles. They are holy convocations, memorials of God's great acts of salvation in history, symbols of the power of God, and types of the anticipated future fulfillment of God's plan of salvation. For the Christian, the festivals and holy days are annual celebrations of God's power, love and saving grace.[4]

The Holy Days include: The Days of Unleavened Bread, Pentecost, Feast of Trumpets, Day of Atonement, Feast of Tabernacles and The Last Great Day (Leviticus 23:1-38; John 4:45; 5:1; 7:37; 12:12; Acts 2:1; 20:16; 1 Corinthians 5:7-8).

BELIEFS AND PRACTICES REGARDING DEATH

BELIEFS

Death is total unconsciousness - without memory, feeling, knowledge or perception (Ecclesiastes 9:5, 10; Psalm 6:5). Through a resurrection, God will judge all who have lived.

The inheritance of the believer is eternal life in the kingdom of God. This inheritance is reserved in heaven and will be bestowed at the second coming of Christ. The resurrected saints will then rule all nations with Christ in the kingdom of God.[5] (I John 2:25; Romans 8:16-19; Daniel 7:27; I Peter 1:3-5; Revelation 5:10)

Unrepentant sinners are those who, after coming to a full knowledge of God, deliberately and ultimately reject him. Their fate is to perish in the lake of fire. This death is eternal, and the Scriptures refer to it as the second death.[6] (Matthew 10:28; 3:12; 25:41; Revelation 20:14-15)

PRACTICES

The Bible does not, nor does the Church specify a particular mode of burial.

SPECIAL RELIGIOUS RITUALS WHICH CAN BE PERFORMED ONLY BY AN AUTHORIZED REPRESENTATIVE OF THIS FAITH

Ordination, anointing of the sick and weddings may be performed only by ordained Church elders.

SACRED WRITINGS REQUIRED

The Holy Bible

SACRED OBJECTS REQUIRED

None

SYMBOLS

During the Lord's Supper or New Testament Passover service, the bread and wine are used to represent Jesus Christ's broken body and shed blood.

SCHOOLS AND INSTITUTIONS

The Worldwide Church of God operates Ambassador University, a 4-year liberal arts university in Big Sandy, Texas U.S.A..

ENDNOTES

1   We're Often Asked ..., (Worldwide Church of God, USA, 1994: 15 pages), p.1-2
2   Statement of Beliefs, (Worldwide Church of God, USA, 1993: 11 pages), p.3
3   We're Often Asked ..., p.3
4   Statement of Beliefs, p.8
5   ibid, p.10
6   ibid, p.10

This chapter was provided by:
Mr. Tito Naman
Personal Correspondence Department
Worldwide Church of God
P.O. Box 44, Station A
Vancouver, British Columbia
V6C 2M2
1-800-663-2345

Many of the subjects discussed in this chapter are covered in brochures produced by the Worldwide Church of God. All literature published by the Church is sent free upon request.

HARE KRISHNA

THE INTERNATIONAL SOCIETY FOR KRISHNA CONSCIOUSNESS

FOUNDER

A.C. Bhaktivedanta Swami Prabhupada

NATURE OF RELIGION

Monotheistic. ISKCON is a worldwide community of devotees practicing bhakti-yoga, the eternal science of loving service to God, practiced in India at least for the last five thousand years.

SCRIPTURES

The Vedas, particularly the Bhagavad-Gita and the Srimad-Bhagavatam. The Vedas deal with the process of devotional service to God as well as with different arts and sciences.

BASIC BELIEFS

The following eight principles are the basis of the Krishna consciousness movement.

- By sincerely cultivating a bona fide spiritual science, we can be free from anxiety and come to a state of pure, unending, blissful consciousness in this lifetime.

- We are not our bodies but eternal spirit souls, part and parcel of God (Krishna). As such, we are all brothers, and Krishna is ultimately our common father.

- Krishna is the eternal, all-knowing, omnipresent, all-powerful and all-attractive Personality of Godhead. He is the seed-giving father of all living beings, and He is the sustaining energy of the entire cosmic creation.

- The Absolute Truth is contained in all the great scriptures of the world. However, the oldest known revealed scriptures in existence are the Vedic literatures, most notably the Bhagavad-Gita, which is the literal record of God's actual words.

- We should learn the Vedic knowledge from a genuine spiritual master - one who has no selfish motives and whose mind is firmly fixed on Krishna.

- Before we eat, we should offer to the Lord the food that sustains us. Then Krishna becomes the offering and purifies us.

- We should perform all our actions as offerings to Krishna and do nothing for our own sense of gratification.

- The recommended means for achieving the mature stage of love for God in this age of Kali, or quarrel, is to chant the holy names of the Lord. The easiest method for most people is to chant the Hare Krishna mantra:

HARE KRISHNA, HARE KRISHNA, KRISHNA KRISHNA, HARE HARE
HARE RAMA, HARE RAMA, RAMA RAMA, HARE HARE

MODE OF WORSHIP

- Our traditional system of Deity worship dating at least five thousand years ago and currently practiced by millions of people today.
- Chanting of the holy names of the Lord, specifically the Hare Krishna mantra.

STRUCTURE

The society is managed internationally by a Governing Body Commission consisting of senior, spiritually advanced members, meeting annually in Mayapur, India. The local management is conducted by a temple president and temple board consisting of congregational members.

DIVISIONS/DENOMINATIONS

None

RITUALS

Please refer to the section entitled *Special Religious Rituals which can be Performed Only by an Authorized Representative of this faith,* located near the end of this chapter.

LAWS

At the time of spiritual initiation members take vows to abstain from the following activities:

- Eating of meat, fish and eggs
- Intoxication
- Gambling
- Illicit sex (sex outside of marriage).

Following these rules helps one to advance in devotional service to God.

MODE OF DRESS/MODESTY REQUIREMENTS

Traditional dress:

- Men's wear consists of lower and upper garments called the dhoti and kurta respectively.
- Women wear a sari (call your local Indian fashion store for further information).

The founder, Srila Prabhupada, has requested his followers to dress as gentlemen and ladies. According to circumstances members sometimes wear traditional dress and sometimes a casual but clean attire.

DIETARY REQUIREMENTS

Please refer to the section entitled *Laws* above.

HOLY DAYS/FESTIVALS

- Sunday Feasts are held at temples worldwide. Programs include such activities as classical Indian dance and music, philosophical discussions and free vegetarian feasts.
- With a few exceptions, each month has its own special festival, such as Janamastami, Gaura Purnima, Vyasa Puja etc.

- A very special annual festival is Ratha Yatra - Festival of Chariots, also known as the Festival of India. It takes place in many major cities of the world and originates in India, where it has been held for at least two thousand years. In Toronto the Festival occurs in July and includes a parade on Yonge Street and a two day celebration on Centre Island. During the Festival of India Hare Krishna devotees distribute an average of twenty thousand plates of free vegetarian food.

BELIEFS AND PRACTICES REGARDING DEATH

BELIEFS

We are not these bodies, but eternal spirit souls, part and parcel of God (Krishna). Right now we are encaged in a material body, which has a beginning and an end. We however, do not die. When one body wears down and dies, we pass on to another body. If we have become fully conscious of Krishna, we do not acquire another material body, but go to the spiritual world, where we reassume our original spiritual form free from birth, death, old age and disease and engage directly in the eternal and ever blissful pastimes of the Lord.

PRACTICES

Devotees perform a ceremony which includes chanting of the Hare Krishna mantra. Bodies are either cremated or buried.

SPECIAL RELIGIOUS RITUALS WHICH CAN BE PERFORMED ONLY BY AN AUTHORIZED REPRESENTATIVE OF THIS FAITH

Samskaras (sacraments) including birth, spiritual initiation, marriage etc.

SACRED WRITINGS REQUIRED

Please refer to the section entitled *Scriptures*, above.

SACRED OBJECTS REQUIRED

Japa (meditation) beads, neck beads, brahminical thread, etc.

SYMBOLS

The Hare Krishna mantra:

HARE KRISHNA, HARE KRISHNA, KRISHNA KRISHNA, HARE HARE
HARE RAMA, HARE RAMA, RAMA RAMA, HARE HARE

ORIGINS

The Hare Krishna movement was brought to the West in 1965 by Srila Prabhupada. However, it has existed in India for at least five thousand years. A very important figure in the history of the movement is the great saint Sri Caitanya Mahaprabhu, who lived in the sixteenth century. The disciplic succession from which the Hare Krishna movement originates was named after this saint, called the Gaudia Vaishnava disciplic succession. Thus, the Hare Krishna movement is an authorized spiritual movement representing the ancient Vedic ideas. The Hare Krishna congregation in Toronto consists of about one thousand families, many of which come from east Indian origin, and whose ancestors have practiced Krishna consciousness for many generations.

This chapter was written by:
Nanda-Tanuja Das
ISKCON Toronto
243 Avenue Road
Toronto, Ontario
M5R 2J6
(416) 922-5415

HINDUISM

FOUNDER

Hinduism does not have a founder. One of the oldest religions, Hinduism evolved through millennia.

NATURE OF RELIGION

Monotheistic; God manifests Himself or Herself in several forms.

SCRIPTURES

- The Vedas is the sourcebook of the Indo-aryans (Hindus)

- The Upanishads form the concluding portion and contain the wisdom of the Vedas

- The Gita (the cream of the Upanishads)

- The Ramayana

- The Mahabharata

- The Puranas

BASIC BELIEFS

- A wide variety of beliefs held together by an attitude of mutual tolerance. All approaches to God are valid.
- Humankind's goal is to break free of this imperfect world and reunite with God.
- The soul reincarnates and transmigrates until reunion with God.
- Many Hindus are vegetarians as the killing of living creatures is not favoured.
- One must perform his or her duties to God, parents, teachers and society.

MODE OF WORSHIP

- Worship occurs in a Temple or at home.

- One must be barefoot during religious worship or any kind of religious celebration.

- One must sit at a lower elevation than where the image of the deity has been placed.

STRUCTURE

Hinduism is not a church-based religion. Therefore, there is no hierarchical structure within the religion.

DIVISIONS/DENOMINATIONS

A Hindu generally belongs to one of 5 major divisions of the religion. One is either a Saiva, a Vaishnava or a worshipper of Ganapati, Sakti or Surya (the Sun). The individual also belongs to a particular Veda - Rik, Sama or Yajuh. Some Hindus are followers of Kartikeya (Muruga). Therefore, daily religious practice is not uniform in all parts of India. The duties and prayers however, are basically the same from north to south. Duties are prescribed from morning until night to cultivate one's moral nature by developing love, kindness and charity.

Hinduism does not have a watertight compartmentalization between the various divisions. Little friction exists between believers of different schools. Each worshipper of a particular manifestation pays due obeisance to the others. Thus, a follower of Vishnu first pays obeisance to the other manifestations before the formal worship of Vishnu begins.

RITUALS

Specific performance of sacraments varies according to local customs in different parts of India. (None of the sacraments signifies a conversion into the Hindu fold or a denomination of it.) The sacraments are as follows:

Nomenclature (Naming of a child):

On the tenth or eleventh day after a child's birth, the priest performs the nomenclature ceremony, invoking the blessings of Gods and Goddesses. (Many Hindus defer the performance to a later date.)

Mundan (First hair cut):

The traditional custom is to shave the child's head on this occasion.

Initiation:

Boys of priestly families are initiated by age 15, entitling them to perform their priestly duties. A second initiation may be performed according to their spiritual capabilities and mental constitution. The second initiation is open to every Hindu at some point of life.

Marriage:

Marriage is a step toward spiritual perfection.

Frequently, with the consent of the bride and groom, marriage is arranged by parents whose duty is to see that children are well established for the second stage of regular family life, the stage of householdership (garhasthya ashram), that follows the restraint and celibacy of student days (brahacharya ashram).

Consulting of horoscopes for match-making is common.

The auspicious day and time of marriage is determined after consulting the almanac.

Tolerance and adjustment are emphasized in marriage.

Divorce is rarely accommodated as an alternative.

Marriage is considered to be as much between families as between individuals. Marriage is performed by having the bride and groom walk around the sacrificial fire seven steps together (fire is looked upon as pure and the light it emits is symbolic of wisdom that dispels the darkness of the mind). By holding the bride's hands, the groom accepts her responsibilities.

Tying a knot of the couple's upper garments is an important part of the ceremony.

The bride's veil adds to her charm and grace. The groom also puts on a head cover.

Kissing does not occur anywhere in the ceremony. Kissing takes place in privacy, for a personal relationship is not expected to be marred by public viewing.

The general sign of marriage for a woman may vary from place to place. In North India it is a vermilion mark along the parted hair on the forehead, while in South India the custom is to wear a sacred thread with special beads (mangal sutra) around the neck or wrist.

Tarpan (Oblations to forefathers):

The whole fortnight during the waning moon period, ending with the dark moon and preceding the Navartri festival is the time when men remember their dead forefathers, offering them water with black sesame seeds.

On the last day, the priest and brahmins are treated with special food.

LAWS

Hindu laws are situationally flexible. Hindus aim to relate holistically to everything living and non-living, including inanimate objects.

MODE OF DRESS/MODESTY REQUIREMENTS

There is no specific requirement other than an emphasis on cleanliness.

DIETARY REQUIREMENTS

There are two types of dietary restrictions, depending upon whether or not a Hindu is a vegetarian:

Restrictions for a Vegetarian Diet

- No meat, fish or eggs, or products thereof.
- Vegetarian and non-vegetarian foods must not be cooked together.
- Milk and milk products are part of the vegetarian diet.
- Under very exceptional situations one might choose to eat *uncooked* vegetables only.
- If one has "dedicated" a specific fruit to God, one is forbidden to eat it for the rest of one's life.
- During occasions like bereavement, a combination of fruits, raw and steamed vegetables (the only cooked food, generally eaten once a day) is acceptable with milk. Rock salt is appropriate for such occasions.

Restrictions for a Non-Vegetarian Diet

- No beef, pork, and possibly eggs or products thereof.
- These must not be cooked with food meant for consumption by a Hindu.
- Otherwise, restrictions are the same as those for vegetarian Hindus.
- A non-vegetarian Hindu will be a vegetarian at special occasions, such as sacraments and special worship events.
- On special occasions a Hindu may fast, eating only fruit and milk or juice.
- Some Hindus abstain completely from alcohol, even in cooking.

HOLY DAYS/FESTIVALS

Festivals are observed at home; some take place in a temple. Hindu festivals occur on the basis of a lunar calculation guided by a solar constraint. All dates are approximate.

Makar Sankranti/Pongal: January 14
Celebration of Spring.
Homage is paid to the Sun, upon whom all life depends, on the occasion of His "ascent" to the north (Uttarayan).

Shivaratri: January - February
A 24 hour celebration including fasting, in praise of Lord Siva.

Holi: February - March
A festival to celebrate the triumph of good over evil.
Huge bonfires are lit at night to commemorate the burning of demoness Holika who perished herself while planning to burn alive a devotee of Lord Vishnu.
It is also a festival of colours, celebrating the sport of Lord Krishna with His devotees.
People meet new friends and revive old friendships on this occasion.

Ram Navami: March - April
Celebration of Lord Rama's birth, who was an incarnation of Lord Vishnu.
The story of Rama is chanted continuously for 24 hours.

Raksha Bandham: July - August
This is a Hindu sister's day.
On this day a sister ties a sacred thread on her brother's wrist and the brother promises to love and help her.

Onam: August - September
A 10 day festival in South India, celebrating the advent of Lord Vishnu in the form of a dwarft (vaman avatar).

Janmashtami: August - September

Lord Krishna's birthday, who was another incarnation of Vishnu.

Krishna was born at midnight, therefore religious services continue until midnight.

Ganesh Chaturthi: August - September

A day to honour Lord Ganesh, the presiding deity of all Hindu worship.

Navaratri: September - October

Continuing for 9 consecutive nights in praise of Lord Rama, it is the longest Hindu festival.

Continuous chanting of the story of Rama, along with evening performances from anecdotes of His life, are held for all 9 days.

The last 4 days are associated with the worship of Goddess Durga (Durga Puga), to celebrate the victory of good over evil. The Goddess is the female principle of energy of the universe.

Dussera/Vijaya Dashami: September - October

10 days following the end of Nava Ratri festival marks the death of demon Ravana at the hands of Lord Rama.

This is also the day of Goddess Durga's parting from Her devotees.

Deepavali (Diwali):   October - November

Festival of light on the new moon day following Dussera. This celebrates Rama's return to Ayodhya after rescuing Sita from Ravana.

Bhratri Dvitiya, or Bhai Dooj: October - November

This is the Hindu brother's day.

On the second day after Diwali, sisters honour their brothers, offering them sweets.

In return, brothers give gifts to their sisters.

BELIEFS AND PRACTICES REGARDING DEATH

BELIEFS

- The atmosphere around the dying person must be peaceful.

- The last thoughts or words are of God, ensuring rebirth to a higher form.

PRACTICES

- Hindus prefer to die at home, as close to mother earth as possible (usually on the floor or ground).

- The Gita is recited to strengthen the dying person's mind and provide comfort so that he or she may begin the final journey.

- Married women's nuptial thread or amulets on the neck or arm, indicating special blessings, should not be removed until just before death. Then, anything which binds the body (such as a belt or ring) is removed, paving the way for the soul's free journey to infinity.

- Nobody should have any attachment to the dead body.

- The family washes the body. The oldest son arranges for the funeral and cremation before day-break.

- Embalming or beautifying the body with artificial decorations is strictly forbidden.

- Sandalwood paste may be used at the occasion.

- White flowers and white clothing (for men only) are appropriate, since white represents peace and purity.

- The body *must* be attended until cremation.

- The names of God (Rama Krishna) and Shiva are chanted, or the Gita is read continuously in the presence of the body. This practice is considered to be very soothing for the departed soul and helpful for the soul's journey back to its source.

- A post-mortem of the body is not favoured.

- Before the cremation, closest relatives should not eat any cooked food.

- Cremation takes place on the day of death. The ashes are usually scattered on water.

- Children less than 2 years old are not cremated, but buried. Usually, no rituals are observed with such infants.

BEREAVEMENT

- After the funeral, taking a bath is appropriate.

- For two weeks, men grow their hair and beards, and dress in white clothes.

- Once a day, unmarried daughters, sons and nearest relatives eat cooked vegetarian food.

- The two weeks of mourning are concluded by the *Shraddha*, a worship event which emphasizes the concept of *peace.*

- Small balls of cooked rice with clarified butter and black sesame seeds (pinda) are symbolically offered to the deceased.

- Men shave their hair and beards.

SPECIAL RELIGIOUS RITUALS WHICH CAN BE PERFORMED ONLY BY AN AUTHORIZED REPRESENTATIVE OF THIS FAITH

- Nomenclature (the naming of a child at birth)
- Marriage
- Initiation vows
- Rituals at death and bereavement
- Important religious occasions

SACRED WRITINGS REQUIRED

- Vedic Prayers
- Upanishad
- Bhagavad Gita
- The Mahabharata
- The Ramayana

SACRED OBJECTS REQUIRED

The following objects are required for performing rituals:

- Sandalwood (for making paste)
- A flat stone piece for rubbing the wood
- Incense
- Water
- Candle or oil lamp
- Fresh flowers
- Food for offering

The following objects are required for Private Worship:

- A private space for meditation.
- A picture or symbol of the chosen ideal.
- A choice to observe fasting on special days.
- A Hindu may wish to observe other special days in consultation with the priests of his or her lineage.

SYMBOLS

The symbol used to represent Hinduism is 'Om', a Sanscrit term for the Supreme Reality or God, taken from the Vedas.

BOOKS

For further information, refer to *Hinduism, A Way of Life*. Sitansu S. Chakravarti. Motilal Banarsidass Publishers PVT Ltd., New Delhi, 1991. ISBN 81-208-0899-1. This book includes a chapter about Hindu pastoral care and chaplaincy.

For further information please contact the following temples (names of contact individuals will change):

1. Swami Pramathananda
Vedanta Society of Toronto*
(For general consultation)
650 Meadows Blvd.
Mississauga, Ontario
L4Z 3K4
(905) 566-5775

2. Pandit Loknath Prashad
223 Cinrickbar Drive
Etobicoke, Ontario
M9W 6W4
(416) 798-2635

3. Mrs. Rina Chakravarti
Multifaith Council Representative
3187 Morning Star Dr.
Missisauga, ON
L4T 1X3

4. Mr. Venkat Raman
79 Thorncliffe Park
Champlain Towers, #207
Don Mills, Ontario
M4H 1L5
(416) 425-8720 Res;
(416) 965-0908 Off.

5. Mr. Surinder Dutt Sharma
Hindu Prarthana Samaj
62 Fern Avenue
Toronto, Ontario
M6R 1K1
(416) 536-9229

6. Bharat Sevashram Sangha
Swami-in-Charge
2107 Albion Road
Rexdale, Ontario
M9W 5K7
(416) 798-0479

* (Branch of Ramakrishna Math and Ramakrishna Mission, India)

This chapter was created from material provided by:
Dr. S.S. Chakravarti
Hindu Community
3187 Morning Star Drive
Mississauga, Ontario
L4T 1X3
(905) 677-7857

ISLAM

FOUNDER

Muhammed (upon Whom be God's peace and blessings) was the name of the Prophet through whom the religion of Islam was revealed. The Prophet Muhammed was born in Mecca, Saudi Arabia around the year 540 (Christian Era). His father 'Abd-Allah died before his birth and his mother, Aminah, died when he was about six years old. The Prophet died in the year 633.

NATURE OF RELIGION

Monotheistic. In Arabic, Islam means peace, purity, obedience and total submission and commitment to the one and only God, and to His laws. Islam, therefore, describes an attribute; the attribute of submission to the will of God.

A Muslim is anyone who has this attribute of "Islam", ie. anyone who submits to the will of Almighty God. Subsequently, Islam is not founded by anyone. "Muhammadanism" is a misnomer of Islam and offends its very spirit. Muslims are not Muhammadans. They do not worship Muhammad. They worship Almighty God. The word "Allah" is the roper name of God in Arabic.

SCRIPTURES

The primary sources of knowledge in Islam are:

- The Quran is the word of God (Allah) revealed through the Angel Gabriel to the last Prophet and Messenger of God, Muhammad (peace be upon him), for the guidance of all mankind.

- The Hadith are the traditions of the Holy Prophet Muhammad. They are also commonly reffered to as his Sunnah. These are his teachings, sayings and actions. These traditions are recorded in the books of Hadith.

BASIC BELIEFS

There are five PILLARS OF ISLAM. These are:

1. Declaration of Faith

   To bear witness that there is none worthy of worship except Allah (Almighty God), and that Muhammed is His Prophet and Messenger to all human beings until the Day of Judgement.

2. Prayers (Salaah)

   To establish Prayers five times daily as a duty towards Allah. They strengthen the relationship with Allah and inspire man to a higher morality. They purify the heart and prevent temptation towrads wrong-doings and evil.

3. Fasting

   To observe the Fast during the Holy Month of Ramadan. During this time Muslims abstain from food, drink, sexual intercourse, and evil intentions and actions. Fasting aims to train the Muslim to live a complete life of total submission to Almighty God.

4. Zakaah

To pay the Annual Charity. It is 2.5% of one's net savings for the year and serves to purify the wealth of the giver and to improve the well-being of the receiver (poorer sections of society).

5. Hajj - Pilgrimage

To perform Pilgrimmage to the Holy City of Makkah once in a lifetime, if one can afford the means of the journey.

Seven ARTICLES OF FAITH

There are Seven Articles of Faith in Islam. These Basic Beliefs shape the Islamic way of life.

1. Belief in the Oneness of Allah

One God, Supreme and Eternal, Creator and Provider, Merciful and Compassionate. God has no father or mother, no sons or daughters. He has not fathered anyone nor was He fathered. None is equal to Him. He is God of mankind, not of a special tribe, race or group of people. He is the God of all, the believers and non-believers of all races and colours. God is Mighty and Supreme, but He is very near to the pious, thoughtful believers; He answers their prayers and helps them. God asks us to know Him, to love Him and to follow His law for our own benfit and our own salvation.

2. Belief in the Angels of Allah

Angels are purely spiritual beings created by God.

3. Belief in the Revelations (Books) of Allah

Muslims believe in the Revelations sent by Almighty God to His Prophets and Messengers.

4. Belief in the Prophets of Allah

All Messengers and Prophets of God were mortal human beings endowed with Divine Revelations and appointed by God to teach mankind to submit to His will and obey His Laws.

5. Belief in the Day of Judgement

Muslims believe in the Day of Judgement and in Heaven and Hell.

6. Belief in Predestination (Qadar)

Almighty Allah has knowledge of and control over everything.

7. Belief in Resurrection after Death

   After the world ends people are brought back to life (Resurrected) to face the Judgement of Almighty Allah.

There are some additional Beliefs Islam teaches. These include:

1. The purpose of life is to worship God by knowing Him, loving Him and by following His Laws in every aspect of our life. Worshipping God does not mean we spend our entire lives in constant seclusion and absolute meditation. To worship God is to live life according to His Laws, not to run away from it.

2. Every person is born free from sin and endowed by God with spiritual potential and intellectual inclination that make him a good Muslim. Salvation can only be achieved through the grace and guidance of God, with faith and good deeds.

3. A Muslim believes that man enjoys an especially high ranking staus in the hierarchy of all the creations of Allah. Man occupies this distinguished position because he alone is gifted with rational faculties and spiritual aspirations as well as freedom of choice and powers of action.

4. A Muslim believes that every person is born a "Muslim". Every person is endowed by Almighty God with spiritual potential and intellectual abilities that can make him a good "Muslim", i.e. someone who submits to the Will of God and obeys Him.

MODE OF WORSHIP

In Islam, worship is an active part of daily life.

- Five obligatory daily prayers (Salaah) at dawn, noon, mid-afternoon, sunset and evening. These can be performed at home, workplace, outdoors or in a mosque; individually or in congregation.

- An obligatory weekly Friday noon congregational prayer is held at the mosque (Salat-ul-Joma). A sermon is given during this time.

- Requirements of Islamic prayers: performing ablution (Wudu) which is washing with water the hands, the face, wiping the head, and washing the feet, purity of the whole body, clothes and ground used for prayer, dressing properly and facing Makkah. If water is unavailable or its use would endanger the health, Taymmun replaces Wudu and is done by striking the hands on pure earth and passing them over the face and the hands up to the elbows.

- Obligatory Fasting (Seyam), occurs once a year during Ramadan, the ninth month of the lunar Islamic calendar. Islamic daily fasting requires complete abstention from eating, drinking, intimate sexual contacts and smoking from the break of dawn until sunset. The fast is broken at sunset.

- Charity Giving (Zakah).

- An obligatory pilgrimage (Hajj) to Mecca occurs at least once during one's life-time. This journey is mandatory for every Muslim man or woman. (Exceptions are made if a Muslim's physical, mental or financial condition makes such a trip impossible.)

- Voluntary acts of worship (in addition to those descibed above).

Prayer Room

- In hospitals and other public institutions a prayer room for Muslims should be provided. The room should be quiet, clean and carpeted. Islamic reading material including the Quran, audio and video tapes should be provided. The direction of Qiblah should be determined and marked in the room, with help from the local Islamic Centre or Mosque.

STRUCTURE

DIVISIONS/DENOMINATIONS

Muslims belong to one of the two main Schools of Islam; the Sunni School or the Shia' School. The majority (over 90%) of Muslims belong to the Sunni School. The basic difference between the two is that the Shia' School believes in the necessity for a spiritual leader and strong authoritative powers, hence a religious structure. The Sunni School on the other hand, does not necessarily require such structure.

Each local Muslim Community, Sunni or Shia', has one or more religious leaders (with formal Islamic education or with self-learned Islamic knowledge). These leaders are often referred to as Imam, Director of the Islamic Centre, or Khateeb (Sermon-Giver).

RITUALS

In addition to the prescribed prayers, a Muslim expresses gratitude to God and appreciation for His favours and asks for His mercy all the time, especially at the times of childbirth, marriage, going to or rising from bed, leaving and returning home, beginning a journey or entering a city, riding or driving, before and after eating or drinking, harvesting, visiting graveyards and at times of distress, sickness and death.

Birth:

- After childbirth, the Call of Prayer (Adhaan) is recited softly in the right ear and the Prayer Commencement Call (Iqaamah) is recited in the left ear.
- Male infants are circumcised.

- A dinner reception and a prayer of Thanksgiving and Gratitude to Allah ('Aqeeqah) is held with relatives and friends.

Marriage:

- Nikaah is the function performed to marry two Muslims, one male and one female.
- After a marriage ceremony, conducted by a qualified Muslim, a reception (Waleemah) is held where relatives and friends are invited.

LAWS

- Islamic laws distinguish among (i) Halal, that which is permitted by God the Law-Giver, (ii) Haram, that which is absolutely prohibited, and (iii) Makruh, that which is considered detestable, but to a lesser degree than Haram. Anyone who engages in Haram is liable for God's punishment, as well as legal Islamic punishment.

- The basic principle in Islamic law is that all things and actions are Halal except those which are specifically prohibited by God.

- Every thing or action which is Haram is very harmful to the individual and/or the group.

- Good intentions do not make any Haram action acceptable.

- Doubtful things are to be avoided.

- Whatever leads to Haram is in itself Haram.

- God has prohibited (as Haram) killing (except for capital punishment), stealing, robbing, consumption of any intoxicant, all types of gambling, sex outside of marriage, all types of pornography and prostitution, homosexuality, wasteful spending and consumption, interest on money (usury), bribery, spreading gossip and backbiting. Additionally singing, music, movies, TV, books, or magazines which promote any Haram are prohibited.

- Smoking is Haram (prohibited) or Makruh.

- Marriage is a religious duty for all who are capable of meeting its responsibilities. Each member of the family has rights and obligations.

MODE OF DRESS/MODESTY REQUIREMENTS

In Islam, clothing has two purposes; to cover the body and to modestly beautify one's appearance. Men are to dress modestly, not imitating women. Women's clothing must cover all of the body including the head, and should not be tight or transparent.

DIETARY REQUIREMENTS

For a Muslim, there are two types of food and drink; Halal (lawful) and Haram (unlawful). **The unlawful, forbidden (Haram) food and drink includes:**

- Meat from dead animals that died naturally through accidents, or by strangling, falling, beating or killed by wild animals.

- Blood that poured forth (as distinguished from the blood adhering to flesh or organs).

- Flesh of swine such as bacon or pork, including all products and by-products (lard, pepsin, gelatin etc.) prepared from swine. Only vegetable oil is used for frying and in preparation of bread, salad dressing, desserts, muffins, etc..

- Food upon which any other name has been invoked besides that of God.

- Intoxicants including all types and varieties of alcohol and intoxicating drugs.

The lawful (Halal) food includes:

- Meat from an Islamically slaughtered animal which does not feed on meat, with the exception of pigs, which is Haram. Examples of such lawful animals are cows, sheep and goats.

- The meat of an Islamically slaughtered bird which does not feed on meat, such as chicken and ducks.

- All seafood from rivers, lakes, seas or oceans as long as the water is not polluted.

The Islamic method of slaughtering an animal or bird takes the following steps:

- First, the Muslim mentions God's name as a reminder that God has command over the life of all creatures. Taking life from an animal or a bird is done by God's permission for the sole purpose of food.

- The animal is slaughtered with a sharp knife; the neck is to be slit from vein to vein with a minimum of pain to the animal. The blood must be drained completely.

- Halal meat (meat of animals or birds, Islamically slaughtered) is widely available fresh, frozen or processed. Contact your local mosque or Islamic Centre.

- Halal Meals: there are several places where Halal meals are sold. Please inquire at the local Islamic Community.

HOLY DAYS/FESTIVALS

Friday is the Muslim holy day. Muslims join together at noon in a congregational prayer at the mosque. Muslims may work on Fridays, except during the time of that prayer which includes a Khutbah (sermon) by a local prayer leader (Khateeb or Imam). Muslims do not believe that God rested on that day or any other day, nor does He ever get tired.

Muslims have two main yearly celebrations (EID):

- Eid-ul-Fitr (the celebration of ending the month of fasting) which is the first day of the lunar Islamic month of Shawal (the 10th month following the month of Ramadan, the month of observing the daily fast).

- Eid-ul-Adha (the celebration of Sacrifice) in remembrance of the intention of Prophet Abraham to sacrifice his son, Prophet Ishmael. This occurs on the tenth day of the twelfth lunar Islamic month of Zul-Hijja. It also marks the end of the Hajj rituals (the Pilgrimage to Makkah).

During these two celebrations, Muslims do not work. They go to mosques, and visit friends and relatives. On these days, Muslims are happy and thankful for God's bounty, and ask for His continued Mercy and Blessings.

Aside from the two Eid celebrations, there are other special days on the Islamic calendar.

Islamic days are based upon the Islamic lunar calendar. The lunar calendar is 11 to 12 days shorter than the Gregorian solar calendar. Thus, the Islamic days are advanced 11 to 12 days each year with respect to the Gregorian solar calendar. The Islamic calendar atarted from the year the Prophet Muhammad migrated (Hijrah) from Makkah to Madinah (623 C.E.).

BELIEFS AND PRACTICES REGARDING DEATH

BELIEFS

Humans consist of a body and a soul or inner-self (Al-Rouh or Al-Nafs). The soul has the ingredients to be both good and bad, and it is up to man to direct it either way. At the moment of death the soul separates from the body. The soul feels God's rewards or punishments and is kept in a transitional state (Barzakh) until the Day of Judgement, the Day of Resurrection.

Humankind is not created in vain. One is held accountable for one's faith, actions and the blessings which God gives in this life. God implements this accountability on the Day of Judgement. Those with a good record will be generously rewarded, showered with God's mercy and warmly welcomed to God's Heaven. Those with a bad record will be fairly punished and cast into Hell. The real nature of Heaven and Hell are known to God only, but God describes them in familiar human terms in the Quran. The time of the Day of Judgement is known to God and God alone.

PRACTICES

As the moment of death approaches, the person (if he or she can), should recite (with help from others) the Islamic Creed (Shahadah) (La Ilaha Illa-Allah Muhammadur Rasuulullaah), meaning "there is no god but Almighty God (the word is Allah in Arabic) and Muhammad is His messenger". A Muslim near the dying person should recite some chapters from the Quran, especially Surah Ya-seen (Chapter 36), and ask God for Mercy and Forgiveness for the dying person.

After death, the individual's eyes should be gently shut, his or her mouth closed with a bandage running under the chin and tied over the head, and arms and legs straightened. The surrounding people can grieve and shed tears but are forbidden to wail, beat the breast, slap the face, tear their hair or garments, or complain or curse.

Ghusl: With minimum delay the body should be thoroughly washed, shrouded and buried. If possible, washing (Ghusl) is performed by a close Muslim relative or friend, but may be performed by any other Muslim who knows the procedure. A man can wash a man and a woman can wash a woman, except in the case of husband and wife, where the husband can wash his wife and the wife, her husband. After washing, the body is shrouded in white cloth sheets.

A funeral prayer (Salaatul Janaazah) is held for the deceased by the local Muslim community, asking for God's Mercy and Blessings. Preferably, this prayer service is held in congregation, and lead by a close relative of the deceased. Any Muslim who knows how to perform it may do so.

As soon as the prayer is over, the body should be taken on a bier to the graveyard for burial. The grave should be positioned so that the body, when turned on its right side, faces Mecca. The body is gently lowered into the grave with respect and dignity. If it is feared that a portion of the body might be exposed while lowering (especially if it is a woman), then a curtain is used. The grave is filled with earth, starting from the head. Every person helps, using both hands. Finally, water should be sprinkled over the covered grave.

The Muslim community condoles, sympathizes and supports the bereaved family and prays for forgiveness of the deceased.

SPECIAL RELIGIOUS RITUALS WHICH CAN BE PERFORMED ONLY BY AN AUTHORIZED REPRESENTATIVE OF THIS FAITH

- Eid-al-fitr Prayer Service
- Eid-al-Adha Prayer Service
- Rituals for the Deceased; Final rites, washing and shrouding of the corpse, Prayer Service.
- Funeral

SACRED WRITINGS REQUIRED

- The Holy Qur'an

SACRED OBJECTS REQUIRED

- Prayer mats, a rug or towel.

SYMBOLS

Not Provided

INSTITUTIONAL CARE FOR MUSLIM GIRLS AND WOMEN

PRIVACY

- Only female doctors, nurses, aides, technicians, etc. should deal with Muslim girls and women in hospitals. Only in life or death situations is the rule waived.
- Only women can share the hospital room or ward with the Muslim patient.
- Privacy should be carefully observed (knock on the door, announce your arrival, etc.).
- Hospital gowns should be long, with long sleeves. If such clothing is unavailable, Muslim women should be allowed to use their own gowns.
- Privacy should be observed during examination, massage, etc., only exposing necessary parts of the body. The rest of the body is covered.

DELIVERY

- If the husband cannot be present, a female friend or relative should be allowed to attend.
- Only cotton pads should be provided.

ABORTION

- The general rule is that abortion is forbidden in Islam. Abortion is only allowed in Islam if the life of the mother is at great risk. Islamic counselling should be made available to Muslim girls and women in all cases where abortion is seriously considered.

EMERGENCY

- In case of emergency, try to get help from a female Muslim doctor. If not possible, then see a female doctor. If not available, see a male Muslim doctor and if one is not available, then accept aid from a male non-Muslim doctor.

TERMINALLY ILL MUSLIM PATIENTS

- Patients should be counselled through local Mosques, Islamic Centres or a knowledgeable Muslim from the local or nearby community.

- Islam does not allow euthanasia or mercy killing and considers it a crime.

For further information please contact your nearest Mosque, Islamic Centre or local Islamic Organization;

or:

Sheik Faisal Abdur Razak
Executive Director
Forum for Islamic Studies of Canada
P.O. Box 36002, 9025 Torbram Road
Brampton, Ontario
L6S 6A3
Telephone: (905) 458-7142
FAX: (905) 793-9872

Mr. Muhammad Yakub Khan
20 Rothsay Avenue
Etobicoke, Ontario
M8Z 4M1
Telephone: (416) 259-2130

Dr. Mohamed Ibrahim Elmasry
402 Clairbrook Crescent
Waterloo, Ontario
N2L 5V7
Telephone: (519) 746-7928

Mr. Mohammed Badran
11 Autumn Hill Cr.
Kitchener, Ontario
N2N 1K9
Telephone: (519) 747-0231 (24 hr. pager)

Council of Imams of Canada
9025 Torbram Road, Box 36002
Brampton, Ontario L6S 6A3

JAINISM

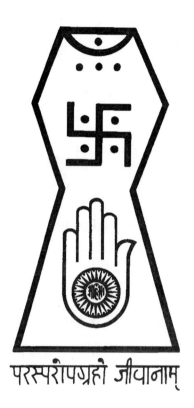

परस्परोपग्रहो जीवानाम्

FOUNDER

Jainism can be considered to be founded by several Jinas (men who have conquered the endless cycles of life and are enlightened) such as Lord Mahavir. Many more Jinas will exist in the future. Jainism has existed from time immemorial.

NATURE OF RELIGION

Jainism provides a system of thought and a way of life.

SCRIPTURES

Many holy books and sutras, for instance:

- Tatvarth Sutra
- Kalpasutra
- Samaysar

BASIC BELIEFS

Jainism rests upon four "pillars":

Ahimsa: Non-violence, ranging from an act of simple kindness to a comprehensive outlook of universal fraternity.

Anekantavada: Principle of relativity, since truth has many aspects, and all viewpoints are tenable.

Aparigraha: Non-acquisition, or setting limits to one's desires so that one does not deny others.

Karma: Deeds or actions, seen as something which accumulates according to one's thoughts and activities and which affects one's future lives.

MODE OF WORSHIP

- Worship takes place in a temple, centre or home.
- The most important prayer is the Namokar Mantra.

STRUCTURE

- The Sangha (Jainist community) consists of Sadhu (monks), Sadhvi (nuns), Shravak (laymen) and Shravika (lay women).
- There is no hierarchical structure.
- Rituals and ceremonies are performed by any knowledgeable person.
- All communities operate independently.

DIVISIONS/DENOMINATIONS

Shwetamber: Shwetamber monks wear white clothes.

Digamber: Skyclad monks. They do not wear any clothes or jewelry, but live skyclad, or in the nude.

RITUALS

Samayika: A 48 minute time of prayer, meditation, and the reading or recitation of sutras from holy books.

Pratikraman: A 50 minute time for one to sit still and review, confess and repent of past and present actions and thoughts.

Snatra Pooja: A worship service of the Tirthankaras (Jinas) using their idols (Murtis).

LAWS

Jainist laws (Panch Mahavrat) for monks and nuns are as follows:

- Ahimsa (Non violence)
- Satya (Truth)
- Asteya (Non Stealing)
- Bramhacharya (Celibacy)
- Aparigraha (Non-Possession)

Jainist laws (Panch Anuvrat) for lay-men and lay-women are observed with limitations.

MODE OF DRESS/MODESTY REQUIREMENTS

- Loose, cotton clothing is worn while performing rituals or religious ceremonies.
- Typical Indian dress is worn at ceremonies.
- Monks and nuns wear unstitched white clothing.

DIETARY REQUIREMENTS

- Jainists are strictly vegetarian.
- Dairy products are allowed.

HOLY DAYS/FESTIVALS

Please note that dates given here are only approximate, as they follow the Jain annual calendar, "Panchang". Please contact the local Jain Centres to determine correct dates during a particular year.

Mahavir Jayanti: **April 13**

The 24th Jina's birthday. Celebrated through prayer and worship in temples. Public functions are held to propagate Mahavir's teachings.

Paryushana Parva: **September 2-9 (in 1994)**

An 8 day festival. Mahavir Janma Vanchan occurs on the fifth day, when Mahavir's life story is read from the Kalpasutra. Samvatsari falls on the last day, the year's holiest day, marked by fasting, meditation, prayers, confession, forgiving and pardoning. It is also the day of universal forgiveness.

Deepavali (Mahavir Nirvana):   November 3 (in 1994)

The day when Lord Mahavir attained salvation, also known as Diwali (the Festival of Light). Celebrated by worship in the morning and illumination (using Deepak) at night. The original event occurred in 527 B.C. at Pavapuri, Bihar, India.

BELIEFS AND PRACTICES REGARDING DEATH

BELIEFS

Jainists believe in rebirth, by which one's soul lives again and again, through many lives in different bodies.

PRACTICES

After death, the body is cremated according to Jain ritual.

SPECIAL RELIGIOUS RITUALS WHICH CAN BE PERFORMED ONLY BY AN AUTHORIZED REPRESENTATIVE OF THIS FAITH

None

SACRED WRITINGS REQUIRED

The Namokar Mantra. This is a general prayer that states our respect for all individuals who have reached a higher spiritual state. It is prayed on all occasions (as is the Lord's Prayer in Christianity).

SACRED OBJECTS REQUIRED

Objects required for Worship Pooja are:

Asta Dravya, 8 items consisting of:

- Pure filtered water.
- Rice
- Chandan (sandalwood and saffron paste)
- Flowers
- Coconut
- Deepak (a lamp)

- Incense
- Dry fruit or nuts such as almonds.

Objects required for Samayika and Pratikraman are:

- A piece of woolen cloth to sit upon.
- A cotton handkerchief.
- A string of 108 beads (mala).
- A particular religious book.

Objects required for Meditation are:

- A mat or piece of woolen cloth to sit upon.
- A peaceful, quiet place to meditate.

JAIN SYMBOL DIAGRAM (SYMBOLS)

The diagram outlines a Jain universe. The swastika represents the four states in which the soul may live: divine, human, tiryanch (animals, birds, plants, etc.), and hell. The three dots represent right knowledge, right vision (faith), and right conduct. The half-moon is the sign of Siddha-Sheela (final place for liberated souls).

The raised hand indicates the principle of non-killing and non-violence. Drawn in the hand's centre is a wheel, representing the propagation of the religion.

This chapter was compiled by:
Mrs. Bhadra Kothari
3956 Glamis Court
Mississauga, Ontario
L5L 3N5

For more information, please contact:
Jain Society of Toronto
48 Rosemeade Avenue
Etobicoke, Ontario
M8Y 3A5
(416) 251-8112

JEHOVAH'S WITNESSES

FOUNDER*

Charles Taze Russell founded the Jehovah's Witnesses in the late nineteenth century. They were known as the "Bible Students". In 1931 they adopted the name "Jehovah's Witnesses".

NATURE OF RELIGION

Monotheistic

SCRIPTURE

The Bible

BASIC BELIEFS*

- Jehovah's Witnesses reject the idea of a holy trinity. God is the Father, while Jesus Christ is His son, and a separate persona. The holy spirit is the name given to God's motivating force.

- Death is a state of total unconciousness.

- Only 144,000 of Jesus faithful apostles will reign with him in heaven.

- Other faithful Witnesses will live forever in paradise on the restored earth.

MODE OF WORSHIP

- Jehovah's Witnesses hold meetings 3 times a week in local Kingdom Halls.

- There are three weekly meetings which include Bible teachings, Theocratic Ministry School and Small group study in private homes.

- Men are designated as elders, or overseers.

- Meetings are not ritualistic but focus on divine education.

- No collections are taken.

STRUCTURE

A clergical class and special titles are considered improper.

DIVISIONS/DENOMINATIONS*

There are no denominations. All Jehovah's Witnesses everywhere in the world hold the same beliefs and worship in the same way.

RITUALS

Adult Baptism by immersion identifies one as a minister of God.

LAWS

Not Provided

MODE OF DRESS/MODESTY REQUIREMENTS*

While there is no specific mode of dress, Witnesses are expected to dress neatly and modestly.

DIETARY REQUIREMENTS

From the time that God allowed flesh to be eaten as food, He commanded: "Its blood - you must not eat." (Genesis 9:3,4) Blood is not to be used as food and when withdrawn from a body it is to be poured out on the ground (Leviticus 3:17; Deuteronomy 12:16, 23, 24). In harmony with the decision handed down by the apostles and older men in the first century, Jehovah's Witnesses' chief concern is to avoid food that contains blood (Acts 15:19, 20, 28, 29; 21:25). Thus, true Christians today avoid eating meat with blood left in it, or other foods to which blood has been added. Clearly God does not object to His people using animal products for food as long as His law respecting blood is obeyed.

HOLY DAYS/FESTIVALS

Once each year on the anniversary of Jesus Christ's death, all Jehovah's Witness congregations celebrate the Memorial of Christ's sacrificial death, or the Lord's Evening Meal (I Corinthians 11:20, 23-26). This is the most important meeting of the year for Jehovah's Witnesses. When Jesus instituted the celebration he commanded, "Keep doing this in remembrance of me."(Luke 22:19)

Matthew 26:26-30 outlines in Jesus' own words the way the Memorial should be celebrated. It is not a ritual with mystical overtones, but rather a symbolic meal, shared by those who have been called to be fellow heirs with Jesus Christ in his heavenly Kingdom (Luke 22:28-30). All dedicated Christians and interested persons are encouraged to attend to show their appreciation for what Jehovah God and Jesus Christ have done for them.

It was on the fourteenth day of the Jewish month Nisan, the date of Passover, that Jesus directed his followers to commemorate his death (Luke 22:14-20). The date is determined by counting fourteen days from the new moon nearest the spring equinox (March 21 and 22) as it would be at Jerusalem in the land of Palestine. Generally, this calculation causes the Memorial celebration to fall each year fall on the date of the first full moon following the spring equinox. Therefore, the actual calendar date varies from year to year.

BELIEFS AND PRACTICES REGARDING DEATH

BELIEFS*

When an individual dies, he or she ceases to exist, and there is only unconciousness. For the wicked, this will be permanent. After Armageddon however, Jehovah God will raise all faithful Witnesses to live in his new, perfect world.

PRACTICES*

An elder performs a funeral service for the deceased and the congregation offers comfort to family and friends.

SPECIAL RELIGIOUS RITUALS WHICH CAN BE PERFORMED ONLY BY AN AUTHORIZED REPRESENTATIVE OF THIS FAITH

Not Provided

SACRED WRITINGS REQUIRED

Not Provided

SACRED OBJECTS REQUIRED

Not Provided

SYMBOLS*

Jehovah's Witnesses do not use any symbols, as God stated that his people should not make any carven images, or likenesses.

This was taken from the chapter written for the Multifaith Information Package, 1991, written by:

Canadian Branch Office
Box 4100
Halton Hills, Ontario
(416) 451-8200

* This information was inserted, as it was not provided. The editor apologizes for any inaccuracies that have been recorded.

JUDAISM

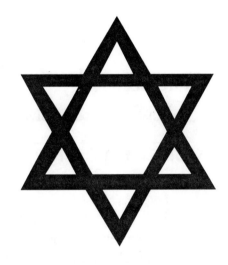

FOUNDER

"Founder" is not an accurate term to describe the origins of the Jewish faith. Jews believe that the Almighty chose Abraham to introduce the concept of Monotheism into a polytheistic world filled with pagan rituals. Thus, God established a covenant with Abraham, Isaac and Jacob and their families, on an individual basis to further spiritual teachings that would be later identified with Jewish theology. The nature of this individual covenant was transformed to one of a national orientation when the Jewish people collectively received the Torah at Mount Sinai. According to our tradition this occurred after Moses led the people to freedom from slavery in Egypt.

NATURE OF RELIGION

Monotheistic

SCRIPTURES

Torah: The Five Books of Moses, Prophets (ethical and ritual responsibilities), Scriptures (ethical and religious values and paradigms).

Talmud: Series of works supplemental to the Torah, outlining and interpreting the laws of the Torah.

BASIC BELIEFS

Existence of one, indivisible God by whose will the universe and all that is in it was created.

MODE OF WORSHIP

- Worship takes place in a Synagogue.

- Jews are required to pray three times daily in a specified manner, at specified times.

- The Jewish Sabbath commences at sundown on Friday and ends at sundown Saturday; candles are lit Friday night and special benedictions are recited over wine and bread; members attend synagogue on Friday evening and on Saturday.

- The Sabbath is a time of rest.

Sabbath Restrictions:	Jews do not work, travel, use electricity, handle money or bathe on the Sabbath.
Havdalah:	The closing ritual for the Sabbath. Rituals may vary but generally they include a candle with 4 wicks, wine, and a spice box.
Phylacteries:	Phylacteries are two small leather cases holding scripture texts, worn in prayer on the forehead and arm. They are used for morning prayers, the Sabbath and during festivals.
Daily Prayers:	Prayers are said twice more during the day; once in the afternoon prior to sunset, and once in the evening after sunset.

STRUCTURE

The Rabbi serves as a religious leader in the community.

DIVISIONS/DENOMINATIONS

ORTHODOX

- Maintain biblical and talmudic regulations.
- Strict observance of the Sabbath.
- Only strictly kosher food (ritually sanctioned) is consumed.
- Modest clothing and head coverings for men and married women.

CONSERVATIVE

- Attempt to abide by talmudic regulations regarding food, Sabbath observance, and festivals.

REFORM

- All religious activity is less rigorous, choice is encouraged.
- English often replaces Hebrew in prayer.

RECONSTRUCTIONIST

- An American movement founded by Mordecai Kaplan which stresses that Judaism is not only a religion but an ongoing tradition and culture.
- Religious rituals are secondary to the cultural aspect.

RITUALS

CIRCUMCISION

- Occurs eight days after the birth of a Jewish male child.
- Symbolizes commitment to the faith of Israel.

NAMING

- On the first Saturday after the birth of any female child a naming ceremony takes place in the synagogue.

PIDYON HA'BEN

- A ceremony of redemption rites which occurs on the 31st day after the birth of the first-born Jewish male.

BAR MITZVAH

- At 13 years of age a Jewish male becomes responsible for fulfilling his own religious obligations. This occasion is marked as the celebrant is called to the Torah in the context of a public prayer service.

BAT MITZVAH

- At 12 years of age Reform and Conservative girls go through a similar ritual as do boys becoming Bar Mitzvah.

MARRIAGE

- This religious ceremony is generally held in a synagogue.
- A marriage contract is written up and signed by the couple.

LAWS

Religious laws exist which govern every area of daily life. However, different groups within the Jewish community ascribe various levels of importance to their observance. (Please refer to the section of this guide entitled *Divisions/Denominations,* above.)

MODE OF DRESS/MODESTY REQUIREMENTS

Orthodox men must have their heads covered at all times, but most men will cover their heads at least during prayer. Most Orthodox men will wear a four-cornered garment with fringes under their everyday clothing. In certain sects men also wear side locks and do not shave. Some Orthodox married women will cover their hair/head when outside the home. Both men and women attempt to dress modestly, with arms and legs covered.

DIETARY REQUIREMENTS

Due to the complexity of this section, it has been placed as the last section of the Judaism chapter. Please refer to it in this location.

HOLY DAYS/FESTIVALS

There are many holy days and celebrations in the Jewish calendar:

ROSH HASHANAH

- Celebration of the new year.
- The time when God judges what will happen to each person in the new year.

FAST OF GEDALIAH

- Death of the last governor of Judea after the Babylonians burned the First Temple in 586 BCE.

TEN DAYS OF REPENTANCE

- The days between Rosh Hashanah and Yom Kippur.
- A time for reflection and repentance.

YOM KIPPUR

- The Day of Atonement, the most solemn holy day of the year.
- Through prayer, people ask for God's forgiveness.
- A day of fast, beginning at sundown the night before and ending at sundown the following day.
- The day on which God's decisions are sealed.

SUKKOTH

- Feast of the Tabernacles; a joyous holiday.
- Nine day harvest festival.
- Many families have their meals and activities in a sukkah (a small temporary booth or hut with a leaved roof, decorated by custom with fruits and vegetables) to commemorate the shelters used by the Israelites when they were being led to the Promised Land.
- Five days after Yom Kippur, Sukkoth is celebrated with special prayers in the synagogue, accompanied with the waving of the citron and the lulav (a palm branch adorned with three myrtle and two willow branches).

HOSHANA RABBA

- Seventh day of Sukkoth.
- Members of the congregation march around the synagogue seven times singing hosannas, the prayers for salvation.

SHEMINI ATZERETH

- Eighth day of Sukkoth, special prayers for rain.

SIMHAT TORAH

- Ninth day of Sukkoth.

- Celebrates the end of the year's Torah readings and recommences from the beginning.

HANUKKAH

- Feast of the Dedication.

- Eight day Festival of Lights to commemorate the Jewish battle for religious liberty led by the Maccabees against their Syrian-Greek overlords.

- Candle lighting ceremonies are observed each night of the festival.

- Small gifts may be exchanged.

ASORA B'TEBET

- A fast day commemorating the beginning of the Babylonian siege of Jerusalem which culminated in the destruction of the first temple, and the people's exile in the year 586 B.C.E.

HAMISHAH ASAR BISHVAT

- A minor festival; the new year of the trees.

FAST OF ESTHER

- Starts the morning of the day before Purim and ends at sundown at the commencement of Purim.

PURIM

- Feast of Lots.

- One day event celebrating the rescue of the Jews of the Persian Empire from destruction.

- The story of Purim is read in the synagogue.

PESACH (PASSOVER)

- Celebration of the exodus of the Hebrews from their enslavement in Egypt.

- Matzot (unleavened bread) is eaten as a reminder of the haste in which they departed from Egypt.

- Dietary Requirements for Passover:

  - No leavened breads or fermented grain products are to be eaten or kept in one's possession on Passover.

- Fresh fruits and vegetables as well as all meat, fish and poultry are the same as usual.

- All other products must be authorized as kosher for Passover.

LAG B'OMER

- A minor festival commemorating the Bar Kochba revolt against Rome.

- It is customary to go on trips and build bonfires.

SHAVUOTH

- Commemoration of the giving of the ten commandments to Moses at Mt. Sinai.

- It is customary to eat dairy products and to stay up late studying the Torah.

SHIVA ASAR B'TAMMUZ

- A fast day commemorating the first breach in Jerusalem's walls by the Babylonians, leading to capture of the city, destruction of the temple, and exile of the Jewish nation from their land.

TISHA B'AV

- A major fast observed on the date (9 Av in Hebrew) that the Babylonians destroyed the First Temple in Jerusalem in 586 B.C.E.. This is also the exact date that the Romans destroyed the Second Temple in Jerusalem in the year 70 C.E.. On both occasions the Jewish people were driven into exile and dispersed among the world's nations. The loss of national sovereignty was seen religiously and theologically as a divine repudiation of the nation's improper observance of God's commandments. The fast commemorates both disasters, and the subsequent exile of the Jewish people.

BELIEFS AND PRACTICES REGARDING DEATH

Practices of death seek to honour the dignity of the body, to assist the bereaved through a process which uses laws of the whole mourning ritual, and to affirm the basic belief that life and death are part of God's plan.

BELIEFS

Jews believe that every human being is composed of a soul (an inner spiritual essence), as well as a corporeal component (the body). When death occurs both the soul and the body return from whence they came; the soul returns to the Almighty in heaven and the body returns to the dust of the earth.

PRACTICES

- The burial should take place as soon as possible, preferably within 24 hours or as soon as the family can be gathered.

- The body must not be left unattended from death until burial.

- Jews are opposed to most autopsies.

- The body must be buried, not cremated.

- Amputated members must be buried, not destroyed.

BEREAVEMENT

- A 7-day period of mourning for the immediate next of kin (Shiva), during which the family receives visitors and gifts of food.

- Jews observe thirty days of social withdrawal with one year of official mourning.

- The Sabbath is not included in the mourning.

- Specific services of remembrance occur after death and at the unveiling of the tombstone.

SPECIAL RELIGIOUS RITUALS WHICH CAN BE PERFORMED ONLY BY AN AUTHORIZED REPRESENTATIVE OF THIS FAITH

All Jewish rituals may be performed by an educated lay person. However, in our society today, considerable discrepancy exists concerning how one defines an educated lay person. Thus, it is customary to have a rabbi officiate in a formal capacity whenever a ceremony is required, to ensure that proper Jewish practice is followed.

SACRED WRITINGS REQUIRED

Please refer to the section entitled *Scriptures*, above.

SACRED OBJECTS REQUIRED

While specific items are ascribed to have a certain amount of holiness (for example; Torah scrolls, phylacteries, prayer books etc.), no objects are venerated or prayed to in the Jewish faith.

SYMBOLS

The predominant symbol of Judaism is the six-pointed star of David.

DIETARY REQUIREMENTS

The Hebrew word kosher means fit or proper as related to dietary (kosher) laws. It means that a given product is permitted and acceptable.

The sources for the laws of Kashruth are either of Biblical or Rabbinic origin. Rabbinic rulings are preventative measures added to the Biblical regulations.

Although there are many complicated details, the main principles of Kashrut are relatively simple. Basically, one must be certain to begin with ingredients that are Kosher, and then ensure that foods prepared from these supplies are made in a manner that maintains this status.

All fresh fruits and raw vegetables are Kosher. The Jewish dietary regulations begin when we deal with foods which derive from animals, fish or fowl. Furthermore, all packaged and prepared foods must be certified Kosher.

Animals
The basic rule here is that any mammal is Kosher, provided it has split hoofs and chews its cud. (See Leviticus, Chapter 11, Verses 2 to 3, 7 to 8, or Deuteronomy, Chapter 14, verse 6.) Thus, cows, sheep and goats are Kosher, whereas pigs (which have split hoofs but which do not chew their cud) are not.

Fish/Seafood
In order to be Kosher, a fish must have fins and scales (Leviticus 11, verses 9 to 12). Examples of Kosher fish are tuna, salmon, carp, trout, bass and pickerel. A catfish, which has fins but not scales, is not Kosher. Other types of seafood such as lobster, shrimp, crab and squid are also not Kosher. Amphibian animals such as frogs and turtles are not Kosher.

Fowl (Birds)
The rules about fowl are not that simple since the types of bird or fowl which are not Kosher are specifically listed in the Bible (Leviticus 11, verses 13 to 20 or Deuteronomy 14, verses 11 to 20). Examples of Kosher fowl are chicken, goose and duck.

Packaged or Prepared Foods
If a certain type of food is not Kosher, it is still not permitted to be eaten when combined with other foods; that is why one must be careful about either packaged or prepared foods containing a non-Kosher ingredient. Thus, for example, it is not permitted to eat cookies which contain non-Kosher animal shortening.

Wines and Cheeses
Although they do not fall into the foregoing categories, all wines and cheeses must be prepared in accordance with the Jewish dietary laws, and must have rabbinical certification in order to be Kosher.

FOOD PREPARATION OR PROCESSING

Jews begin with Kosher ingredients, but there are still rules with regard to Kosher preparation. Some examples of these rules are as follows:

Ritual Slaughter

Before a cow or any Kosher warm-blooded fowl or animal may be eaten, it must be slaughtered in accordance with Jewish law. In order for an animal to be slaughtered as Kosher, this must be done by an experienced ritual slaughterer in the proper manner (Deuteronomy 12, verses 20 - 21).

There is a rule that even a Kosher type of animal must be healthy. Accordingly, the ritual slaughterer will examine the internal organs, such as the lungs of the animal, before the meat of the animal may be eaten. If he can see a mortal wound or infection on the organs of the animal, its meat may not be eaten.

Removing Blood and Fat

After the animal is properly slaughtered, it must be processed in a way which will extract the blood from its meat. Jews are not permitted to eat certain animal sinews and fats. Since it is quite difficult to separate the Kosher meat from the sinews and fats in the hind quarters of the cattle, most Kosher meats come only from the front quarters.

SEPARATION OF DAIRY AND MEAT

It is generally known that you are not permitted to mix milk with meat foods. In fact, you are not allowed to cook milk and meat together in one cooking utensil, nor can they be eaten together at the same time. This is based on a text repeated in the Bible several times (Exodus 24, verse 19; Deuteronomy 14, verse 21).

Food products containing milk or dairy products should not be eaten for several hours after consuming food products which contain meat or meat derivatives.

PASSOVER

For the holiday period called "Passover" which lasts just over one week and which usually occurs in April of each year, extra Kashrut rules apply in addition to the usual ones. At this time, the all year cooking vessels and tableware are not used, and Kosher homes go through a full change-over to Passover utensils (one set for dairy purposes, the other for meats, as usual), for the holiday period. This is to avoid all leavened foods during the holiday (Exodus 12, verses 33 to 34, 39; Chapter 13, verses 6 to 8; Leviticus 23, verses 4 to 6). Disposable (one-use-only) plates and containers are frequently used at this time of year.

Since Kashrut on Passover can be pretty complicated, it is common to seek direction from local Rabbis or Jewish Chaplains. Even Jews who are not very religious try to keep up with the Passover rules, which are considered very important. Besides Matzas (flat, unleavened bread wafers), many other special Kosher products are sold especially for Passover. (Of course, these foods can still be used after the holiday.)

UTENSILS

The taste of hot foods is absorbed into most utensils, such as metal pots and pans or ceramic tableware. For example, if you put hot chicken on a clean plate, the plate will absorb the flavour of the chicken.

After removing the chicken, one may not use that plate for dairy products because the flavour previously absorbed into the plate will mix with the milk product, which is not allowed.

This is why observant Jews have two entirely separate sets of dishes, as well as pots and pans, for each of milk and meat foods. Foods which contain no milk or meat ingredients (i.e. eggs or fish) are "neutral" or "pareve" and can be used with milk or meat utensils. Another possibility is to use disposable, one-use-only cups, flatware and plates; airlines use this method to accommodate their Kosher-eating passengers.

CERTIFICATION

Any prepared or packaged foods which contain non-Kosher ingredients are also not Kosher. That is why Kosher consumers search for a Rabbi's certification that the product is Kosher, or they do a careful review of the ingredients in the product to ascertain that it is Kosher. This is sometimes hard to know, even for experts; ingredient lists may not provide all the information needed to know for sure what is Kosher.

Most food products which may contain non-Kosher ingredients need rabbinical certification. In Canada, the two main bodies which provide such certification are; the Congress Orthodox Rabbis ("COR") which is given by the Canadian Jewish Congress in Toronto, and the Kashrut Council of Montreal ("MK"). If you see either the COR or the MK symbol on the outside of the package, the food product is Kosher. The most common Kosher symbol on foods from the U.S.A. is the O-U.

Foods which require Kosher certification that are to be consumed later or at a different location, are wrapped and sealed with the certification affixed in such a way as to ensure that it will only be removed immediately before consumption. For example, Kosher food packages on airlines are enclosed in silver paper and sealed with tape, with the Kashrut certification stamped on the tape. The certification is valid only until the seal is broken or the package opened. Thus, it is important that the wrapping remain intact.

For more information, telephone the Canadian Jewish Congress, Kashrut Department, 4600 Bathurst Street, Willowdale, Ontario (416) 635-9559, or Chaplaincy Services at (416) 638-7800.

We gratefully acknowledge Rabbi L. Davids, Rabbi S. J. Steinberg, and Rabbi R. Weiss as the authors of this chapter.

For more information contact:
Director
Chaplaincy Services
Toronto Jewish Congress
C.J.C. Ontario Region
4600 Bathurst Street
Willowdale, Ontario
M2R 3V2
Phone: (416) 638-7800

THE CHURCH OF JESUS CHRIST OF LATTER-DAY SAINTS (THE MORMONS)

FOUNDER

The Church of Jesus Christ of Latter-day Saints was organized according to New York State law on April 6, 1830 in Fayette County, New York, U.S.A., by Joseph Smith Jr. and five others. In answer to a fervent prayer, prompted by a biblical scripture (James 1:4-5), Joseph Smith Jr. was personally visited in 1820 by God the Father, and the Son, Jesus Christ, who told Joseph to join none of the existing churches. Members believe that a number of angels visited Joseph over the next ten years instructing his activities, which included translating the golden plates found on a hill near Palmyra, New York, left on the American continent by the Lord's prophets in about 400 A.D.. These golden plates were translated into what members now accept as *The Book of Mormon, Another Testament of Jesus Christ*. From this book the church received its nickname, "The Mormons".

NATURE OF RELIGION

Our faith is totally centred and focused on Jesus Christ as:

- The Firstborn of God, born of the virgin Mary, and the resurrected son of an Eternal and Living God, the Eternal Father.

- The creator of the heavens and the earth.

- The Jehovah of the Old Testament, the Christ of the New Testament.

- The head of the church today.

- The source of all latter-day revelation via his chosen prophet, the president of the Church of Jesus Christ of Latter-day Saints.

- He who atoned for all humankind's sins, and He who is the personal Saviour of all who repent and call upon His name, and obey His commandments.

Members believe that they are literally the spiritual sons and daughters of a living Father in Heaven who loves and cares for each of his children, more so than mortal parents can love and cherish their own children. Followers believe that mortality is a probationary period during which they are in "school", being tested to see if they will obey the commandments which the Lord has given through the prophets, and fulfill those requirements necessary to return to the Celestial Kingdom, a kingdom where one is exalted and where God the Father and God the Son reside, the highest kingdom spoken of by Paul in his first epistle to the Corinthians.

Members believe that personal agency is a vital ingredient of mortality, and a gift of God who created human beings in his own image. Salvation, or being "saved", members believe, is God's gift for all humankind, provided by Jesus Christ's Atonement. "Exaltation", however, must be earned by going beyond one's profession of a belief in Christ and by doing good works, helping one another with the gifts and talents that mortal men and women were given, and by living all of God's commandments, given through the prophets, both ancient and latter-day. Members also believe that whatever knowledge they attain in mortality will be carried with them into the realms of eternity.

Mormons are a covenant people, building temples, as did Moses and Solomon of old, where sacred and personal covenants can be entered into with the Lord.

SCRIPTURES

Members accept as canon the Bible, both the Old and New Testaments, and believe that the King James translation is the most correct. Members also believe that the Lord, through the prophet Joseph Smith, accomplished necessary corrections to the many translations made from the original Hebrew and Greek editions. Other scriptures accepted include:

The Book of Mormon, Another Testament of Jesus Christ.

The Doctrine and Covenants, 138 latter-day revelations given since 1820 to enhance members' lives and provide direction regarding how the Lord wants His church directed.

The Pearl of Great Price, writings of Abraham, Moses, and Joseph Smith.

All the latter-day counsel relating to the church spoken from the lips of the latter-day prophets and apostles.

BASIC BELIEFS

While church practice may change according to inspiration received by the current prophet-president (polygamy for example, was abolished in 1890), the basic tenets remain unchanged. In 1842, Joseph Smith summarized them in a concise statement of Mormon beliefs that is still accepted as scripture today. They are known as the Thirteen Articles of Faith:

We believe in God the Eternal Father, and in His Son, Jesus Christ, and in the Holy Ghost.

We believe that men will be punished for their own sins, and not for Adam's transgression.

We believe that through the Atonement of Christ, all mankind may be saved, by obedience to the laws and ordinances of the Gospel.

We believe that the first principles and ordinances of the Gospel are: first, Faith in the Lord Jesus Christ; second, Repentance; third, Baptism by immersion for the remission of sins; fourth, Laying on of hands for the gift of the Holy Ghost.

We believe that a man must be called of God, by prophecy, and by the laying on of hands by those who are in authority, to preach the Gospel and administer in the ordinances thereof.

We believe in the same organization that existed in the Primitive Church, namely, apostles, prophets, teachers, evangelists, and so forth.

We believe in the gifts of tongues, prophecy, revelation, visions, healing, interpretation of tongues, and so forth.

We believe the Bible to be the word of God as far as it is translated correctly; we also believe the Book of Mormon to be the word of God.

We believe all that God has revealed, all that He does now reveal, and we believe that He will yet reveal many great and important things pertaining to the Kingdom of God.

We believe in the literal gathering of Israel and in the restoration of the Ten tribes; that Zion (the new Jerusalem) will be built on the American continent; that Christ will reign personally upon the earth; and that the earth will be renewed and receive its paradisiacal glory.

We claim the privilege of worshipping Almighty God according to the dictates of our own conscience, and allow all men the same privilege; let them worship how, where, or what they may.

We believe in being subject to kings, presidents, rulers and magistrates, and in obeying, honouring and sustaining the law.

We believe in being honest, true, chaste, benevolent, virtuous, and in doing good to all men; indeed, we may say that we follow the admonition of Paul - we believe all things, we hope all things, we have endured many things and we hope to be able to endure all things. If there is anything virtuous, lovely, or of good report or praiseworthy, we seek after these things.

MODE OF WORSHIP

Members worship God the Father through His Son, Jesus Christ, and pray to God the Father also through the Son, Jesus Christ. On Sundays, members gather in a chapel close to their home and partake of the Lord's Sacrament blessed and passed by the Aaronic Priesthood. Spiritual talks are provided by members of all ages and genders. Class lessons based upon the scriptures are provided for all age groups. Men meet together in priesthood meetings (males 12 years old and up hold the priesthood) for social fellowship, to receive gospel instruction, and to report on their assignments. Women meet together for social fellowship, gospel training, and to report on their assignments in the Woman's Relief Society, one of the oldest (organized in 1842) and largest women's organizations in the world.

Twice each year church members gather together in conference to sustain the chosen leaders and to receive instruction from the prophet and apostles on the latest word of the Lord. These meetings are now sent by satellite to members world-wide, being translated instantaneously into the receiver's language. Also, twice each year, members gather at "Stake Conference" to receive special instruction from local leaders and to socialize one with another. Women meet twice a year to receive instruction from their World Relief Society leaders, as do the priesthood brethren, beginning at age twelve.

The primary worship is reserved for the home, which provides all basic instruction. Families are encouraged to dedicate Monday evenings as "Family Home Evenings" where all family members gather together to pray, have fun, read the scriptures, and to be one with another. Daily prayer and daily scriptural reading is encouraged from as early as when a child first learns to talk and read.

STRUCTURE

The structure is highly organized to efficiently manage a world wide church that functions in over 150 nations, with nearly nine million members and 50,000 full time missionaries, yet it is so simple that each individual has personal access to God the Father via the gift of the Holy Ghost. This gift is bestowed at baptism upon every member. The church is organized in much the same way that Jethro, Moses' father-in-law, counselled Moses to organize his flock in the desert, with leaders over certain numbers; 1000, 500, 100, etc. However, the basic organization of the church is the family, with each individual having specific responsibilities, and where the parents, walking side by side, equal in authority, accept the responsibility to people the earth, and to train children in righteousness.

The church's primary purpose is to teach individuals correct principles and how to be Christ-like in their lives, providing them with the proper tools to correctly govern themselves. With these skills, both men and women can build strong marriage and family relationships which in turn builds strong communities and nations.

Church organizations that assist individuals and families to become more Christ-like are:

> The Primary Organization for small children through age 11.
>
> The Young Women and Young Men's Organizations for youth age 12 through 18.
>
> The four year religious seminary program for high school age students.
>
> The religious institute program for college and university age members.
>
> The women's Relief Society for women ages 18 to 100 which presents such diverse programs as "Spiritual Living", "Home and Family Education", "Compassionate Service/Social Relations", and "Home Management".
>
> Men ages 19 to 100 receive priesthood training in subjects that include "Counselling with Your Children", "The Power of Faith in Jesus Christ", "Improving Family Communications", "Teaching Children to Work", "Keys to Effective Leadership", etc.

The basic source of doctrinal training is the Old Testament, the New Testament, the *Book of Mormon*, and church history, including the *Doctrine and Covenants*.

The church does not pay clergy, other than a living allowance for those at the general authority level. At the congregational level, leaders (both men and women) are called from the membership ranks and serve as Bishops, Counsellors, Presidents, Teachers, Clerks, etc., all without pay, aside from the blessings received for serving as a Disciple of Jesus Christ in building His church.

DIVISIONS/DENOMINATIONS

None

ORDINANCES (RITUALS)

The church teaches that all church "Ordinances" (Rituals) must be performed by one who has been granted the authority to perform that particular "Ordinance". All church authority is derived from Jesus Christ, who received His authority from God the Father. The Church

President has been delegated holder of all "Keys of Latter-day Authority" and delegates, as needed, down to lower levels of church ecclesiastical leaders. The church "Ordinances" include:

Naming & Blessing of Children: This ordinance can be performed by any male member who has received the Melchizedek Priesthood. Fathers usually perform this ordinance.

Baptism: Baptism involves totally immersing the believer in water by a member of the priesthood who possesses the authority. The age of accountability for baptism, as defined by the Lord, is 8 years.

Bestowing the Holy Ghost: The Holy Ghost, the Comforter, is bestowed upon all baptized members by a Melchizedek Priesthood member immediately following their baptism.

Priesthood Ordination: A worthy male member is given the "Aaronic Priesthood", or the lesser priesthood, at age 12 and ordained to the office of a deacon. At age 14 he is ordained to the office of a teacher, and at age 16 to the office of a priest. Each office has specifically stated responsibilities, including considerable training and preparation for life. At age 18 a worthy young man is given the Melchizedek Priesthood and ordained an Elder. Each ordination is usually performed by the young man's father, always by a Melchizedek Priesthood member. Other offices in the Melchizedek Priesthood to which an individual can be ordained include Seventy, High Priest, Patriarch, and Apostle. The Melchizedek Priesthood holds the authority to administer in all spiritual matters within the Church of Jesus Christ of Latter-day Saints. Each office has its prescribed authority.

Patriarchal Blessing: A "Patriarchal Blessing" is given to all members, male and female, by the "Stake Patriarch". This blessing is a sacred blessing that provides spiritual and temporal direction for a member's life when followed with faith. This blessing is usually given when members are in their mid teens, or a year after baptism for converts.

Marriage: The church performs two types of marriages, civil and temple.

Civil Marriage: This marriage is performed by a Bishop or Stake President, and is one performed outside the temple. This is a marriage "for time (mortality) only".

Temple Marriage:

This marriage is performed within the walls of a "Holy Temple", and is performed by a Melchizedek Priesthood member set apart as "Temple Sealer," having been given authority to marry, or "seal for time and eternity".

Temple Covenants:

Church members are a temple loving people. Just as the Lord directed Moses and Solomon of old to build temples, so too, members believe, the Lord has directed his latter-day prophets to build temples in our time. Currently in 1994, the church has in operation 46 temples world-wide, including two in Canada, one of which is located in Brampton, Ontario. A properly dedicated temple, also known as "The House of the Lord", is a facility that members may enter to make eternal covenants with the Lord. Covenants are both "sacred" and "holy". Prior to dedication temples are open to the public, following dedication only members who hold temple recommends are able to enter into these holy places.

Members believe that Christ's Atonement was the first vicarious ordinance (doing an ordinance for others who cannot do it for themselves) performed on earth. Following His teachings (see I Corinthians 15:29) and latter-day commandments, latter-day saints perform the required vicarious ordinances in the temples for ancestors who have completed their earthly sojourn without a knowledge of the Lord's gospel fullness. Through vicarious temple ordinances, family generations are linked together as eternal families. Members are encouraged to search out their family ancestors, and record them in the church archives. Millions of non-members use the more than 2,150 "Stake Family History Libraries" located world-wide to search out their own family histories. These families often send their family records to Salt Lake City for permanent storage in the Family History vaults.

LAWS

Mormon laws are to obey all of God's commandments; and to render unto Caesar what is Caesar's, and unto God what is God's.

MODE OF DRESS/MODESTY REQUIREMENTS

Mode of dress follows the members' homelands' varying national and cultural norms and customs.

DIETARY REQUIREMENTS

In 1832, following a prayer for understanding, the Lord revealed to the prophet Joseph Smith Jr. what is known as the Word of Wisdom. It was not given as a commandment, but as counsel to all saints. This Word of Wisdom indicated that tobacco was not for human use, that alcohol was to be used for washing human bodies, not for consumption, and that "hot drinks," later defined to be coffee and tea, were not good for people. The Lord indicated that people were to use meat sparingly, only in times of winter, cold or famine, and that all fruits and herbs were for their use, as were all grains, saying specifically "nevertheless wheat for man." The Lord closed this revelation by stating that all who would follow this counsel "shall find wisdom and great treasures of knowledge, even hidden treasures; and shall run and not be weary, and shall walk and not faint."

Today, for members to obtain a recommendation to enter the Lord's Temple, they must indicate that among other things they do not smoke, drink alcoholic beverages, use "drugs", tea or coffee.

HOLY DAYS/FESTIVALS

Mormons follow basic Christian holidays such as Christmas and Easter, as well as national holidays for members' home nations. Additionally, the following holy days are specific to the church:

> April 6th is celebrated as Christ's true birth and the church's anniversary, organized in 1830.

> Pioneer day is celebrated every July 24th as the day "the Saints" arrived in the Salt Lake basin in 1847.

> June 27th is remembered as the day the Prophet Joseph Smith Jr. was martyred in 1844.

BELIEFS AND PRACTICES REGARDING DEATH

BELIEFS

The church teaches that all individuals will be resurrected, and will attain the degree of glory in heaven for which they were qualified while living in mortality, while those who never heard of Jesus Christ in mortality will be taught Christ's Plan of Salvation in the "spirit prison" which Paul spoke of in his epistle to the Hebrews. To move out of this prison, individuals must accept the Lord's Plan of Salvation, and accomplish their basic mortality work by proxy. This will be the millennium's primary work. Paul taught the Corinthians this very plainly, and the prophet Malachi relates to this teaching in his Old Testament book, chapter 4.

PRACTICES

Upon death a member is given a Christian burial. The burial plot is dedicated as the body's final resting place until the first resurrection, when it will be reunited with the spirit. Members who received their "Temple Ordinances" will usually be buried in their "Temple Robes" (special clothing worn when they obtained their ordinances).

SPECIAL RELIGIOUS RITUALS WHICH CAN BE PERFORMED ONLY BY AN AUTHORIZED REPRESENTATIVE OF THIS FAITH

All temple ordinances, including the sealing of husband to wife, and children to parents, for time and all eternity within the walls of a church temple.

All church ordinances such as baptism, bestowing the gift of the Holy Ghost, patriarchal blessings, etc.

SACRED WRITINGS REQUIRED

None

SACRED OBJECTS REQUIRED

None

SYMBOLS

None

SCHOOLS AND INSTITUTIONS

A fundamental teaching of the church is that "the glory of God is intelligence". The church has established an extensive educational system that includes home, primary, secondary, college and university secular training, intertwined with foundational religion courses for all levels and ages of its members. Brigham Young University (BYU) in Provo, Utah is the church's flagship university which includes a satellite university in Hawaii serving the members located in the "Islands of the Sea". It also operates a large Jerusalem Studies Program, headquartered in Jerusalem. The Church Educational Department operates youth seminary programs, an Institute Program for university aged members and primary and secondary schools in Mexico and in many islands of the Pacific.

ORIGINS

The Church of Jesus Christ originated in the pre-existence. During the great war in heaven, as it was referred to by John the Revelator in his Book of Revelation, chapter 12, a third of heaven's hosts were cast out, along with Lucifer, their brilliant leader. At this point, Jesus Christ presented the Plan of Salvation. This plan provided that "agency, or freedom to choose" was a basic ingredient of mortality, a testing time between human pre-existence and life after life, or eternity; the time when Christ agreed to be humankind's mediator between justice and mercy, to atone for our sins, and to be the world's first resurrected being, providing the way for all to follow Him.

This is the same church organization given to Adam and Eve, to Noah and his children, to Abraham, and was the higher law first given to Moses on Mt. Sinai. Since the Israelites were not yet ready to live this higher law, Moses was given a second set of laws, the lower law, or law of carnal commandments. This is the law that was lived from the time of Moses to the coming of Christ. When Christ began his ministry he "restored" the higher law once again. Following the Apostolic period, compromises were made between the church and civil authorities which caused the Gospel fullness to again be taken from the earth. In 1820 God the Father and His Son Jesus Christ personally visited the teenager Joseph Smith, which led to full restoration of the Lord's Plan of Salvation. The legal organization of the Church of Jesus Christ of Latter-day Saints followed on April 6, 1830. The term "Latter-day Saints" indicates the same Church of Jesus Christ, but "restored" in these "latter-days".

This chapter was written by:
Donald and Joan Conkey
Directors of Public Affairs, Eastern Canada
The Church of Jesus Christ of Latter-day Saints
91 Scenic Millway
Willowdale, Ontario
M2L 1S9
(416) 441-0452

THE REORGANIZED CHURCH OF JESUS CHRIST OF LATTER DAY SAINTS

FOUNDER

Joseph Smith, Jr., born December 23, 1805, died June 27, 1844.

ORGANIZED

April 6, 1830 by Joseph Smith, Jr.

REORGANIZED

April 6, 1860 by Joseph Smith III

NATURE OF RELIGION

Monotheistic, Christian; (The RLDS Church centres its belief and practice in the basic affirmations of the Christian faith.)

SCRIPTURES

The Holy Bible (Old and New Testament). Many versions are used including a revised version by Joseph Smith, Jr. popularly called the "Inspired Version."

Book of Mormon (Like the Bible, a collection of books—fifteen in all—whose central testimony is of Jesus Christ.)

Doctrine and Covenants (A compilation of documents the Church accepts as inspired statements representing a standard of Church law and practice.)

BASIC BELIEFS

We believe...

in God, the source of all love and life and truth.

in the life, death and resurrection of Jesus Christ being incarnate by the Holy Spirit for the salvation of all humankind and the inner meaning and end toward which all history moves.

in the ministry of the Holy Spirit that bears record of God and Christ and is one with them.

in the gifts of the Spirit.

that humanity is endowed with freedom and created to know, to love and to serve God, and to enjoy communion with God.

that salvation is by grace.

that all are accountable to God for managing all gifts and resources given into their care.

in Zion as a concrete implementation of the principles of the Kingdom of God on earth, expressed both in present reality and future hope.

in the call of each person to be a disciple, and in the particular call and ordination of some men and women to priesthood.

that the sacraments witness the continuing life of Christ in the Church.

in continuing self-revelation of God and in an open canon of scripture.

MODE OF WORSHIP

Most RLDS congregations conduct Sunday morning worship services consisting of hymns, scripture readings and a sermon. Anyone may participate in the service with the exception of the performance of Church sacraments which require specific ordination.

STRUCTURE

World Headquarters Organization includes:

The First Presidency, the chief executive officers of the Church.

The Council of Twelve Apostles, concerned with worldwide missionary activities.

The Presiding Bishopric, concerned with Church properties, financial matters and stewardship.

Every two years delegates gather for a World Conference in legislative sessions to define the Church's program and financial affairs. Local congregations are administered by a pastor, two counselors and various assistants. Generally, congregations are grouped into districts, and districts into regions, each administered by a president. A more highly organized composition of congregations in close geographic proximity is called a stake.

PRIESTHOOD

Two orders of priesthood exist within the church structure:

Aaronic with responsibility for the physical and temporal ministries including deacons, teachers, and priests.

Melchisedec containing two sub-divisions; Elders and High Priests (both often referred to as Elders) with spiritual and administrative responsibilities.

The 1984 World Conference of the Church authorized the ordination of women to priesthood which had hitherto been available only to men.

DIVISIONS/DENOMINATIONS

None

SACRAMENTS (RITUALS)

Baptism: The rite of initiation into the Church by immersion in water, usually in a baptismal font in a church sanctuary and witnessed by others in a worship setting. It is performed by priests or elders. Baptism is available for persons 8 years of age or older.

Confirmation: Elders lay hands on the individual's head and pray as representative of God's response to the one who has been baptized. This completes the rite of membership.

Blessing of Children: An infant of a few weeks or months old is brought to the elders who hold the child while one of them offers a prayer of blessing. This may be performed for members or non-members.

Lord's Supper (Communion):	Customarily celebrated the first Sunday of each month. Worshippers kneel while specified prayers are read by priests or elders who then serve the emblems to members or non-members.
Marriage:	May be performed by priests or elders for members or non-members. Civil marriages or marriages performed by other clergy are also recognized.
Administration to the Sick:	An individual's head is anointed with a small drop of olive oil and a prayer offered for that person's welfare. Available to members or non-members.
Ordination:	Performed by the laying on of hands.
Patriarchal Blessings:	Special prayers offered by evangelists using the laying on of hands to members generally above the age of sixteen. The blessing, which is usually given only once, is a request for wisdom and guidance.

LAWS

General application of the Ten Commandments and the Sermon on the Mount guide members' actions as interpreted from an ethical position rather than a legalistic one. In general, members are expected to be of high moral character and in good standing with their church and community. Use of tobacco, alcoholic beverages and non-medicinal drugs is strongly discouraged. Use of these would disqualify a member from serving in the priesthood.

MODE OF DRESS/MODESTY REQUIREMENTS

Not Applicable

DIETARY REQUIREMENTS

Not Applicable

HOLY DAYS/FESTIVALS

The Church follows the general holy days of the Christian calendar.

BELIEFS AND PRACTICES REGARDING DEATH

No special requirements for funeral or burial practices.

SPECIAL RELIGIOUS RITUALS WHICH CAN BE PERFORMED ONLY BY AN AUTHORIZED REPRESENTATIVE OF THIS FAITH

Only the sacraments listed above must be performed by authorized persons (priesthood). All other functions of worship may be performed by either ordained or unordained persons. Church sacraments are performed as part of a worship service and are open to the public.

SACRED WRITINGS REQUIRED

The Church uses what it terms the 'Three Standard Books"; *Bible*, *Book of Mormon* and *Doctrine and Covenants*.

SACRED OBJECTS REQUIRED

Not Applicable

SYMBOLS

The main symbol used in the Church is the peace symbol depicting the lion, child, and lamb.

PEACE

SCHOOLS AND INSTITUTIONS

Graceland College; a four-year liberal arts college in Lamoni, Iowa.

Park College; a four-year liberal arts college in Parkville, Missouri.

Elbert A. Smith Retirement Center, Inc.

Resthaven; an eldercare facility.

Herald Publishing House

Outreach International; a U.S. based third-world development agency.

World Accord; a Canadian based third-world development agency.

Zerin Corporation and Sionito Corporation; Senior Citizen and low income housing in Toronto and London, Ontario.

Camp Quality; a non-denominational camp for children with cancer.

OTHER NAMES

Due to the length of its name, various abbreviations are used, the most common being "RLDS Church" and "Saints Church." In Quebec the Church is known as the Restored Church of Jesus Christ (Eglise Restauree de Jesus Christ). The Church may be known by other names in other countries based on local laws and clarity of translation.

HISTORICAL ROOTS

The RLDS Church originated during religious enthusiasm and revival associated with the Second Great Awakening in America (early 1800's). With a background in Protestant religious tradition, Joseph Smith Jr. laid claim to "restoration" of First Century Church principles and founded a movement in Fayette, New York in 1830 to effect the "restoring" of Christ's church to its original form and authority.

The RLDS Church is traced to the origins of this body established by Joseph Smith in 1830. Upon Smith's death in Illinois in 1844 various persons made leadership claims and took with them parts of the Church, the largest group following Brigham Young to what is now Utah. In 1852 a "new organization" of unattached members began in Wisconsin, and in 1860 Joseph Smith III, son of the founder, accepted leadership of what was to become the Reorganized Church of Jesus Christ of Latter Day Saints.

The RLDS Church has no affiliation with the Latter Day Saints (Mormon) church. Headquarters were first established in Illinois, then Iowa, and are presently located in Independence, Missouri.

MEDICAL PRACTICES

No restrictions

SOME ACCEPTABLE GENERAL SOURCE BOOKS

An Introduction to the Saints Church, Peter A. Judd and A. Bruce Lindgren, Independence, Missouri: Herald Publishing House, 1987.
Exploring the Faith, Alan D. Tyree, ed. Independence, Missouri: Herald Publishing House, 1987.
Who Are The Saints (booklet), Independence, Missouri: Herald Publishing House, 1977.
The Priesthood Manual, Independence, Missouri: Herald Publishing House, 1990.
Our Legacy of Faith, Paul M. Edwards, Independence, Missouri: Herald Publishing House, 1991.

This chapter was written by:
Larry Windland, Ontario Regional President   (519) 822-4150
Reorganized Church of Latter Day Saints
390 Speedvale Avenue East
Guelph, Ontario N1E 1N5

NATIVE SPIRITUAL TRADITIONS

FOUNDER*

Native spirituality does not have a founder, but has evolved over centuries and been passed down from one generation to the next.

NATURE OF RELIGION

Traditional Native cultures are authentic and dynamic, fostering distinctive and sophisticated human development. A sense of identity and pride are rooted in established spiritual traditions and principles.

Native spiritual life is founded on a belief in the fundamental inter-connectedness of all natural things, all forms of life, with primary importance being attached to the land, Mother Earth. A basic sense of community or group contrasts with the non-Indian culture's individualism and sense of private ownership.

There is no distinction between spiritual life and cultural life. For Canadian Natives, spirituality is a total way of life. This spirituality is rooted in the direct experience of a Creator or "Life Force" during individual and group rituals.

SCRIPTURES*

There are no written scriptures, but ceremonies and beliefs are learned by word of mouth and actual experience.

BASIC BELIEFS*

Please refer to the section entitled *Nature of Religion* above. It provides a good description of Canadian Natives' basic beliefs.

MODE OF WORSHIP*

Native spirituality is expressed through ceremony, or ritual. Please refer to the section entitled *Rituals (Ceremonies)* for a detailed description which accurately reflects Native mode of worship.

STRUCTURE (ELDERS)*

Elders may be either women or men. Their most distinguishing characteristic is wisdom, which relates directly to age. One Elder might have the "gift" or power to interpret dreams, another to apply herbal remedies, a third to heal in a sweat lodge. As a rule, no Elder can perform all ceremonies.

DIVISIONS/DENOMINATIONS*

Native spirituality is as diverse as the bands which make up the Canadian Aboriginal People. Geography and community membership determine how Native Canadians worship.

RITUALS (CEREMONIES)

Ceremonies are the primary vehicles of religious expression. A ceremonial leader or Elder assures the authenticity and integrity of religious observances. There is no written doctrine. Teachings are passed on verbally by recognized Elders.

Individuals concentrate on the realism of the inner self, particularly self-to-self and self-to-others. One seeks the four aspects of enlightenment; strength, knowledge, understanding and sharing (which translates into love). Inner conflicts and fears are confronted in an effort to develop mental and emotional truth and honesty, and to remove all conflicts.

PRAYER

Through prayer, a native person communicates daily with the Creator and Spirits. One normally prays with the burning of sweetgrass, sage, cedar or tobacco, the four sacred plants.

THE PIPE

Pipes are used for private and group prayers. Prayers are transmitted through the smoke of burning plant material in the pipe's bowl. The pipe is not a personal possession, but belongs to the community. The holder of the pipe is considered to be its custodian. While every native has the right to hold the pipe, in practice he or she must earn that right. Individual pipe use is normally conducted in consultation with an Elder. Used in a group, the pipe ceremony is a primary group event over which Elders preside, while the participants gather in a circle. It is preceded by the burning of a braid of sweetgrass to purify the worshippers and symbolize unity.

SACRED CIRCLE

This is similar to the pipe ceremony, with the addition of an allotted amount of time for each participant to address the circle, if he or she desires.

FASTING

This is a special form of prayer, one which is attracting growing numbers of participants. An Elder provides the necessary ceremonial setting, and conditions and guides the individual who fasts.

Fasting involves total renunciation of food and water for a number of days specified by the participant. Prior to the fast, an elder and a doctor evaluate necessary health conditions.

SWEAT LODGES

The sweat lodge is another fundamental collective ceremony. It is a purification procedure which precedes spiritual quests. Many lodges are for communal prayer purposes, but others are for healing or "doctoring". Usually, a sweat is required both before and after the fast. An appropriate site is a virginal section of ground which has not been desecrated by the trampling of feet or the disposal of waste matter. After an Elder has selected a site, it will be blessed with tobacco and sweetgrass. Construction details vary from tribe to tribe and can only be dealt with on an individual Elder basis.

It takes about 1.5 hours to erect a 5 foot high, igloo-shaped structure from bent willow branches tied together with twine. The structure is covered with canvas or blankets, to exclude all light. It can accommodate about eight persons at a time.

Stones are heated outside the sweat lodge, traditionally in a fire. Four stones are admitted 4 times each to the sweat lodge, representing the four directions. There are prayers and singing as well as pipe smoking during the 2 hour ceremony.

FEASTING

Some ceremonies, such as a "doctoring" sweat, require a meal. Specific rituals (which call for certain types of food) must be followed.

Sacred foods for the Ojibway (an eastern tribe), are wild rice, corn, strawberries and deer meat. Typical feast food for a Cree from the prairies would be bannock (Indian bread), soup, wild meat and fruit (particularly Saskatoon berries or mashed choke cherries). For an Indian from the west coast, the sacred food might be a kind of fish prepared in a special way. Although foods differ, their symbolic importance remains the same.

LAWS

Not Provided

MODE OF DRESS/MODESTY REQUIREMENTS

Not Provided

DIETARY REQUIREMENTS

Native religious dietary requirements are a function of tradition and environment. Again, Elder approval provides the ultimate legitimizing sanction which is also subject to an institutional Superintendent's approval.

HOLY DAYS/FESTIVALS

Festivals are closely related to seasonal changes, the moon, the provision of food and other living essentials. The Elder usually determines festival dates.

BELIEFS AND PRACTICES REGARDING DEATH

BELIEFS

The after-life is a world of peace.

PRACTICES

- After death, there is often a 4-day wake which includes visiting the body.
- Family, friends and special food are important during the wake.
- A pipe ceremony often follows the funeral service and burial.

SPECIAL RELIGIOUS RITUALS WHICH CAN BE PERFORMED ONLY BY AN AUTHORIZED REPRESENTATIVE OF THIS FAITH

Almost all of the ceremonies previously described must be performed or supervised by an elder who has earned and been granted such responsibilities by recognized others. The most common ceremonies performed in an institutional setting are the Pipe and Purification Ceremonies.

SACRED WRITINGS REQUIRED*

Not Applicable

SACRED OBJECTS REQUIRED

(Please refer to the section entitled *Rituals (Ceremonies)* above, for descriptions of other sacred objects.)

Eagle wings and feathers, rawhide gourds, drums, abalone shells, altar cloths and prints are some of the more common sacred objects used in addition to the pipe. The four sacred plants are also often worn around the neck in a "medicine" pouch.

Eagle feathers are awarded for outstanding deeds. They may be worn in the hair or on a costume, but ordinarily they are carried in the hand. Indians regard the eagle as a sacred bird; the eagle represents power, strength and loyalty.

Drums contain the heartbeat of the Indian nation. There is one size for doctoring purposes and another for ceremonial use.

Rattles are used to doctor the sick. Rattles are shaken to call the spirit of life which takes care of human beings. Rattles are also used during sweat lodge ceremonies. The Elder invites the spirits of the four directions to come in and help participants who are seeking a spiritual and physical cleansing to start a new life.
The burning of sweetgrass, sage or cedar is a widespread, daily private practice for those who are deeply involved in Native spirituality. For these individuals, it should be regarded as normal that they possess at least one braid of sweetgrass for daily devotional use. This practice is usually followed in consultation with an Elder. (It is customary to burn sweetgrass while saying prayers early in the morning or in the evening, before the sun goes down.)

Tobacco, Sage, Cedar, Sweetgrass and Kinikink are sacred elements to the North American Aboriginal People. The Creator gave them to us to pray with. We pray by burning them. We offer the incense of the smoke to the whole of creation, to an individual or to a group of people. (None of the elements are hallucinogenic whether or not they are burning.)

The kinikink is smoked in the Sacred Pipe. Kinikink is concocted by the Pipe Carrier. It is made of various combinations of bark and herbal plants.
Kinikink is rarely used anymore because it is time consuming to make and gathering the necessary materials is difficult. Ordinary tobacco is used instead as it is much more available (as opposed to natural homegrown tobacco which is almost totally unavailable).

The four sacred plants are used in both individual and group ceremonies. Each plant originally was given to a specific tribe, but now they are often used together, either as an incense mixture which is ignited in an abalone shell (or other container) so that the smouldering, purifying material can be passed from person to person, or worn in a medicine pouch.

An Elder provides plant material for the pouch. The one wearing the pouch asks for mercy and protection from the spirits of the four directions. Elders caution individuals not to conceal in their pouches anything other than the sacred plants, as to do so would make a mockery of their beliefs.

Additionally, other herbs and dried animal pieces are used in certain ceremonies. Selection is a matter of tribal tradition and involves consultation with herbalist medicine persons, of whom there are few. Diamond willow fungus, dried and ground beaver testicles and dried buffalo droppings are some of the other materials
which may be burnt.

Elders possess additional personal sacred items. Religious articles carried by Elders must not be touched by anyone other than the elder. If inspection is required, an Elder should be invited to provide inspection services. A woman should not come near sacred objects during menstruation, because related energy cancels the power of such objects.

SYMBOLS*

Native spirituality uses a great variety of symbols which vary from one tribe to another.

SPIRIT VISITATIONS

Native spirituality recognizes Spirit Visitations that require the Elder's attention and ceremonial assistance. "Spirit Visitations" have become more frequent today, but they are always good spirits. It is often necessary visit an individual receiving Spirit Visitations who needs help and advice in that regard. Usually a ceremony is required.

For further information, please contact:

Wandering Spirit Survival School Aboriginal Legal Services of
935 Dundas Street East Toronto, or Native Canadian
3rd Floor   Centre of Toronto
Toronto, Ontario 16 Spadina Road
M4M 1R4 Toronto, Ontario
(416) 393-0555   M5R 2S7
      (416) 964-9087
      (416) 924-2147 (education)

RASTAFARIANISM

ORIGIN (FOUNDER)

Rastafarianism is the religious expression of a spirituality born among the black people of Jamaica during generations of unspeakable oppression and human suffering.

Elements of this spirituality are a protest against the injustice and cruelty afflicted upon the black people by the white establishment, a yearning for deliverance from bondage, for freedom in a new land, the land of their ancestors, Africa. It is a radical attempt to reclaim their African heritage.

a yearning for deliverance from bondage, for freedom in a new land, the land of their ancestors, Africa. It is a radical attempt to reclaim their African heritage.

NATURE OF RELIGION

Not Provided

SCRIPTURES

Not Provided

BASIC BELIEFS

- Blacks are God's chosen people, today's true Hebrews.
- Western Civilization with its white establishment is Babylon, the godless city of evil. The Pope is the head of Babylon who leads the oppression and mental enslavement of the black people.
- The Bible is the Word of God, although some parts of today's Bible are not from God, but originate from God's enemies.
- The police are Babylonian agents, protecting white society by oppressing black people.
- The reward for following the ways of the Bible is "life ever-living" and repatriation to Africa, the land of freedom.
- The Ethiopian Emperor Haile Selassie (who died in 1975) is an incarnation of God, still reigning in the spiritual body through a "High Council" of fifteen men (theocratic government), seated in Jamaica.

MODE OF WORSHIP

- Rastafarians meet weekly for worship.
- Leadership is male and charismatic.
- Women are excluded from spiritual leadership.
- Worship consists of prophecy, Biblical inspiration, music (especially drums), dance and smoking of marijuana.
- The groups meeting for worship are called "circles".

STRUCTURE

Not Provided

DIVISIONS/DENOMINATIONS

Not Provided

RITUALS

SMOKING OF MARIJUANA (CALLED "GANJA")

- This relaxes and opens the mind and soul, enabling God to take over and inspire/illuminate the believer.

- Smoking may be done individually, or may be shared by passing around a ceremonial pipe made of bamboo.

- Ganja is considered to contribute to a person's spiritual, mental and physical health.

- Babylon (the white society) outlaws the smoking of marijuana because of this herb's power to provide healing and access to Truth.

THE GROWING OF "DREADLOCKS"

- This is an expression of a spiritual commitment to the Rastafarian faith and way of life and one's opposition to Babylon and its combs, scissors and razors.

- The longer the hair, the holier the person. The long locks are like the wool of sheep or lambs and, at the same time, like a lion's mane.

- Black people, like Haile Selassie, are simultaneously lambs and lions.

- Rastafarians may wear a woollen "tam", a sort of turban, often in the colours of African liberation; red, black, green and gold.

- The cutting of the locks by police whenever a Rastafarian is apprehended is experienced as an act of abuse and brutality, an assault on the person's spirituality and identity.

LAWS

Rastafarians do not believe in using contraceptives or abortion.

MODE OF DRESS/MODESTY REQUIREMENTS

Not Provided

DIETARY REQUIREMENTS

- Only natural, vegetarian foods are consumed. No meat, fish, eggs or poultry. Rastafarians prefer to drink rainwater, rather than treated water.
- Members abstain from hard drugs or liquor, beer, wine and any other alcohol.
- Some Rastafarians prefer to eat with fingers from a coconut shell, rather than use utensils.
- In every way possible, Rastafarians choose the ways of nature over (Babylonian) civilization. Nature gives life and healing, civilization brings death and destruction.

HOLY DAYS/FESTIVALS

The Annual "Grounation": April 23
A celebration in honour of Haile Selassie and a renewal of one's commitment to live a natural life.

Haile Selassie's Birthday: July 23

BELIEFS AND PRACTICES REGARDING DEATH

Not Provided

SPECIAL RELIGIOUS RITUALS WHICH CAN BE PERFORMED ONLY BY AN AUTHORIZED REPRESENTATIVE OF THIS FAITH

Not Provided

SACRED WRITINGS REQUIRED

Not Provided

SACRED OBJECTS REQUIRED

Not Provided

SYMBOLS

Not Provided

Some of the information about Rastafarians was obtained from an excellent resource,
Rastafari, A Way of Life, by Tracy Nicholas
Anchor Books 1979.

SIKHISM

FOUNDER

Guru Nanak (1469-1539), the first in a succession of ten Gurus, ending in 1708.

NATURE OF RELIGION

Monotheistic

SCRIPTURES

The Guru Granth Sahib, a book of collected religious writings, substitutes for human Gurus since the death of the last Guru in 1708. Therefore, the scriptures as the "Living Word" are treated as the "Living Guru" (teacher).

BASIC BELIEFS

- There is one God, whose name is truth eternal. Creator of all things, the all-pervading spirit. Fearless and without hatred, timeless and formless. Beyond birth and death. Self-enlightened. Known by the Guru's Grace.[14]

- God is the supreme Guru, revealed as guide and teacher through the Word, contained in the Guru Granth Sahib.

- Humankind by nature is ignorant, misguided, and dominated by the evils of lust, covetousness, attachment to worldly things, wrath, pride and egotism. This results in a cycle of birth and rebirth.

- Only God's grace can turn a person from self-centred to God-centred. Human effort can create the conditions for God's grace to be effective. Final liberation depends upon God's grace. Tension exists between God's sovereignty and human free will.

- Salvation is liberation from the cycle of birth and rebirth. One is transformed to a life of truth, contentment, compassion, patience and humble service for God and humanity. Sikhs do not view renunciation or asceticism, including acts like fasting and begging, as a saintly attitude. Sikh religion is intrinsically life-affirming. The ideal is a life of work, worship and charity.

- The equality of all people is expressed by the common name "Singh" for men (meaning Lion) and "Kaur" for women (meaning Princess or Lioness); everyone, regardless of social status, is a lion or a princess. Thus, women in each household have an independent identity.

MODE OF WORSHIP

Sikhs engage in private worship twice daily, in the morning and again at night:

Mornings: Bathing, meditation, recitation of prayers and hymns.

Evenings: Recitation of prayers and hymns; prayers before going to bed.

STRUCTURE

The last Guru, Gobind Singh (who died in 1708), replaced the Sikh community's individual leadership with the collective leadership of the Khalsa, Brotherhood of the Pure. Local leadership consists of an elected committee of five initiated elders.

There is no priesthood, although many gurdwaras have a Granthi who organizes and conducts services. (Gurdwara means church; literally "abode of God".)

DIVISIONS/DENOMINATIONS

There are no denominations or factions among Sikhs.

RITUALS

Naming of a child after birth: A child is named by opening the Guru Granth Sahib at random; the first letter of the first verse on the left-hand page becomes the first initial of the child's name.

Initiation: This involves the baptismal ceremony, performed at any mature age, baptismal anointment, bathing, bearing the 5 Articles of Faith, etc.

Marriage: The vows are taken by the man and woman in the presence of the Guru Granth Sahib, while circumambulating (walking around) the scriptures 4 times. This ceremony is accompanied by marriage hymns.

Death and bereavement: Please refer to the section entitled *Beliefs and Practices Regarding Death*, below.

LAWS

The *Rehat Maryada*, the Code of Conduct, provides guidance for daily living.

MODE OF DRESS/MODESTY REQUIREMENTS

THE 5 ARTICLES OF FAITH

Men and women who have been initiated into the Khalsa bear the 5 articles (the 5 K's):

KESH (uncut hair): Symbolizes spirituality, a commitment to life.

KANGHA (comb): Symbolizes orderliness and discipline in one's commitment to life.

KIRPAN (sword): Symbolizes courage and self-sacrifice as one defends the weak and upholds righteousness.

KARA (steel bracelet on right wrist): Symbolizes discipline and constraint in the use of the kirpan.

KACH (shorts as underwear): Symbolizes rejection of a life of renunciation and asceticism.

Together, these 5 articles of faith signify a way of life, helping the wearer to resist the erosion of one's faith. Additionally, a turban is worn primarily by the male as a symbol of personal sovereignty and responsibility to others.

The Kirpan is the last privilege given to a Sikh, bestowed after the other 4 articles of faith have been worn with honour. Individuals involved in criminal activities lose the right to wear the Kirpan.

DIETARY REQUIREMENTS

- Use of tobacco, intoxicants or alcohol is not accepted.

- Sikhs are generally non-vegetarian.

- Fasting is not accepted as a religious practice, although it can be observed for medical reasons.

HOLY DAYS/FESTIVALS

Sikhs meet in congregation for a prayer service and a common meal on the following primary holidays:

- Guru Nanak's birthday.

- Guru Gobind Singh's birthday.

- Martyrdom of Guru Arjan Dev, who built the Golden Temple at Amritsar.

- Martyrdom of Guru Tegh Bahadur.

- Baisakhi Day (April 13th), the Founding of the Khalsa.

- Investiture of Guru Granth Sahib.

Those attending worship at the Gurdwara remove their shoes and cover their heads before entering the building as a sign of respect for the Living Teacher, the Guru Granth Sahib.

BELIEFS AND PRACTICES REGARDING DEATH

BELIEFS*

Sikhs believe in the spirit's rebirth into a new life, until one achieves final salvation.

LAST RITES (PRACTICES)

- The body is bathed, dressed and cremated.

- In case of a father's death, the oldest son must be present at the cremation and is subsequently recognised as the new head of the household, signified by tying a turban on his head.

- The floor is washed and covered with white sheets; people take their shoes off outside the room.

- A brief service for relatives is held with hymn singing.

- Lamenting is not in order, but members give thanks to God for the deceased's life.

- The body is cremated. Afterward, a service is held at the home or temple, with continuous reading from the Guru Granth Sahib. This lasts approximately 48 hours.

SPECIAL RELIGIOUS RITUALS WHICH CAN BE PERFORMED ONLY BY AN AUTHORIZED REPRESENTATIVE OF THIS FAITH

The rite of Baptism must be performed by the 5 members of the Khalsa.

SACRED WRITINGS REQUIRED

All Sikh ceremonies, celebratory or solemn, revolve around readings from the Guru Granth Sahib.

SACRED OBJECTS REQUIRED

The Guru Granth Sahib alone is central to all Sikh services.

SYMBOLS

Just as the cross symbolizes Christianity and the Star of David the Jewish faith, so does the Khanda symbolize the Sikh religion. Rooted in Sikh history and theology, it reflects certain fundamental concepts of the faith.

The symbol derives its name from the double-edged sword (the khanda) at the heart of the logo. The khanda is a potent metaphor of divine knowledge, its sharp edges cleaving truth from falsehood.

The circle around the khanda is the "chakra" - the perfect figure, without beginning or end, symbolizing God. The Sikh is to seek divine knowledge as the road to ultimate union with God, which is a state as complete and perfect as the circle.

The two swords are the traditional "kirpans". They symbolize the twin concepts of "miri" and "piri" - temporal and spiritual responsibility. They occupy a central place in Sikh theology which places equal emphasis on the individual's spiritual aspiration and upon his or her duty to serve society.

The opposing kirpans in the logo thus represent the balance between personal spiritual salvation and one's obligation to serve others. Godliness governs individual action; at the same time, religious practice must revolve around service to the poor, oppressed and disadvantaged.

[14]   A quotation from the *Mool Mantra*, a summary statement of faith about God, by Guru Nanak.

This chapter was written by:
Mr. T. Sher Singh
10 Deerchase Court
Guelph, Ontario
N1G 3X5
Phone:(519) 836-6565
Fax: (519) 836-5430

*   This information was inserted, as it was not provided. The editor apologizes for any inaccuracies that have been recorded.

UNITARIANS AND UNIVERSALISTS IN CANADA

FOUNDER

The Unitarian and Universalist religions began as movements within Christianity, and appeared at different times in different places. People who believed in universal salvation, or that God is one being, rather than a Trinity, broke off from orthodox groups either because they were deemed to be heretics or when they felt that they no longer belonged. Various people arose as leaders of these movements, but no one person can be identified as the "founder' of our religion.

NATURE OF RELIGION

Although Unitarianism is known primarily for its denial of one Christian doctrine, it covers a much broader spectrum of belief. It is a comprehensive program for religious reform, rooted in humanism and the radical Reformation. It is as much a spirit as a program, stressing free intellectual inquiry, freedom, tolerance, and ethical living.

Unitarian and Universalist views have evolved under the impact of science, philosophy and encounters with world religions. Today there are some Unitarians who describe themselves as theists and others who call themselves humanists. Many feel uncomfortable with labels.

Unitarians do not hold rigid, unquestioned, black and white beliefs. They maintain that all beliefs must be open to question and examination, and may then be accepted, modified or rejected. They affirm that beliefs must be subject to the scrutiny and revision of reason and experience. They reject truth with a capital "T", the truth of a holy book that cannot be questioned or the truth of an authoritative church. Truth is a function of persons, in every age and every walk of life, not of books beyond reason nor of churches beyond doubt.

Unitarians and Universalists are firmly committed to truth with a small "t," to the right - indeed the duty - of personal judgement. Freedom of belief is not a licence for religious anarchy or irresponsibility. It is an opportunity for careful, hard, honest thought. Every person should develop his or her own capacity for personal judgement so that she or he may, in the words of the apostle Paul, "Prove all things; hold fast to that which is good." Nor is it all a private matter; Unitarians believe in sharing personal convictions and beliefs with each other in an atmosphere of openness and mutual respect.

SCRIPTURES

Unitarians and Unitarian Universalists do not regard a particular source as "scripture." We believe that truth can be found in many sources, ancient and modern. While recognizing our Judeo-Christian heritage, we also look to the religious writings of other faiths, to the insights of science and philosophy, and to poetry and literature for guidance and inspiration. The readings in our hymnal, *Singing the Living Tradition*[15], provide a representative sample of the type of religious material which we find meaningful and inspiring.

BASIC BELIEFS

Many Unitarians and Universalists would begin a statement of basic principles with a commitment to "freedom, reason and tolerance," principles which have guided Unitarian thinking from the beginning of its history. From our Universalist roots would come a strong emphasis on love and on developing our spiritual nature.

In 1984 and 1985, the Unitarian Universalist Association, of which all Canadian societies are a part, adopted the following statements of principle:

We, the member congregations of the Unitarian Universalist Association, covenant to affirm and promote:

- The inherent worth and dignity of every person.

- Justice, equity and compassion in human relations.

- Acceptance of one another and encouragement to spiritual growth in our congregations.

- A free and responsible search for truth and meaning.

- The right of conscience and use of the democratic process within our congregations and in society at large.

- The goal of world community with peace, liberty and justice for all.

- Respect for the interdependent web of all existence of which we are a part.

The living tradition we share draws from many sources:

- Direct experience of that transcending mystery and wonder, affirmed in all cultures, which moves us to a renewal of the spirit and an openness to the forces which create and uphold life.

- Words and deeds of prophetic women and men which challenge us to confront powers and structures of evil with justice, compassion and the transforming power of love.

- Wisdom from the world's religions which inspires us in our ethical and spiritual life.

- Jewish and Christian teachings which call us to respond to God's life by loving our neighbours as ourselves.

- Humanist teachings which counsel us to heed the guidance of reason and the results of science, and warn us against idolatries of the mind and spirit.

Grateful for the religious pluralism which enriches and ennobles our faith, we aspire to deepen our understanding and expand our vision. As free congregations we enter into this covenant, promising to one another our mutual trust and support.

MODE OF WORSHIP

There is no set formula or pattern for worship in Unitarian or Universalist societies. Within established churches, worship most commonly takes the form of clergy leading a basic Protestant style of service including music, readings, meditation, and a sermon. Smaller fellowships may have a more informal pattern, and special occasions may include a great variety of religious forms and patterns.

STRUCTURE

Congregational polity is basic to our structure. Societies may choose to have clergy or to be entirely lay-led. Ministers are called directly by the congregation, although the settlement process is facilitated through the Department of Ministry of the Unitarian Universalist Association. Congregational leadership is elected; all societies are required to have by-laws which help provide democratic leadership.

Most societies have Chaplains, lay people who are licensed through the Canadian Unitarian Council and the respective provincial governments to perform rites of passage; weddings, dedications and memorial services.

In Canada, societies are members of the Canadian Unitarian Council, which has as its mission to:

- Be a liberal religious voice in Canada.

- Provide connections and communication among societies and members across Canada.

- Support the development of member societies.

- Support growth of membership in Canada.

Societies are also members of the Unitarian Universalist Association, our continental religious body, located in Boston, Massachusetts.

DIVISIONS/DENOMINATIONS

Unitarians and Unitarian Universalists are very "organizational," and within the Unitarian Universalist Association there are a number of affiliate organizations representing particular perspectives. Those which arise from theological considerations, as opposed to social action or other concerns, include the Fellowship of Religious Humanists, the Unitarian Universalist Christian Fellowship, the Unitarian Universalists for Jewish Awareness, and the Covenant of Unitarian Universalist Pagans. Most Canadian Unitarian Universalists probably would not identify with these groups specifically, although some might. This organizational variety is often reflected within larger Unitarian congregations.

RITUALS

Unitarian congregations do not follow prescribed religious rituals or ceremonies. Many congregations begin their services by lighting the Chalice (please refer to the section entitled *Symbols*, below). Most congregations have developed some form of welcoming ceremony for new members, and may also hold specific services (during holidays for example), which have become important and meaningful to them.

Child dedications, in which the community takes responsibility for the nurture and support of the child and his/her family, are common. Weddings and memorial services are developed with the couple or family, so as to reflect the values and preferences of the individuals involved.

LAWS

There are no laws directing Unitarians or Unitarian Universalists; indeed, that would be inconsistent with our commitment to "a free and responsible search for truth and meaning," and "the right of conscience and the use of the democratic process within our congregations and in society at large." Most of our members very highly value the development of a personal code of ethics and the living out of that code in one's life.

MODE OF DRESS/MODESTY REQUIREMENTS

None

DIETARY REQUIREMENTS

None, although an increasing number of our members are vegetarians, primarily for economic, environmental or health reasons. Most Unitarian gatherings provide vegetarian dishes as a matter of course.

HOLY DAYS/FESTIVALS

Most Unitarian and Universalist societies celebrate Christmas and Easter, although the emphasis is more humanistic and universal than Christian. Societies may regularly celebrate other religious holidays; a Seder is not uncommon in many societies. Thanksgiving services are also characteristic.

The one uniquely Unitarian celebration is the Flower Communion, as developed by Karl Capek, a Czech Unitarian who died in a Nazi concentration camp during World War II. Patterned after a Christian communion, the flower communion is marked by the sharing of flowers; each participant brings a flower to the service, and takes another home.

Rites of passage are important to Unitarians as they are to all religious groups. In child dedications the society joins with the parents in committing themselves to providing the child with a loving and supportive community in which the child can grow up.

Although there are some general guidelines about the content of weddings, couples usually work with the minister or chaplain to ensure that the service reflects their own beliefs and ideas. Services of Union are available to same sex couples.

BELIEFS AND PRACTICES REGARDING DEATH

BELIEFS

Since most Unitarians and Universalists see human life as part of the natural world, they tend not to believe in an afterlife. It would be very unusual to find a Unitarian or Universalist who believed in any kind of a heaven or hell outside of earthly experience.

A commitment to the primacy of personal conscience in religious matters means that Unitarians generally oppose laws which limit such freedom, including laws restricting abortion and the right to die. Many Unitarians actively support "living wills" and patients' rights to refuse treatment or life supports. Some Unitarians would also support individuals' rights to determine the time and manner of their death.

PRACTICES

Unitarians have been at the forefront of the Memorial Society movement in Canada, and generally prefer simplicity in their practices related to death. Cremation of the body is most common and memorial services, without the body present, are the norm. Most memorial services focus upon the person's life, and its impact on other people and the community.

SPECIAL RELIGIOUS RITUALS WHICH CAN BE PERFORMED ONLY BY AN AUTHORIZED REPRESENTATIVE OF THIS FAITH

None

SACRED WRITINGS REQUIRED

None

SACRED OBJECTS REQUIRED

None

SYMBOLS

The flaming chalice has become our symbol, and many congregations light the chalice at the beginning of their services, as well as on other occasions. It combines the cup, symbolizing sharing, generosity, sustenance and love, and the flame, symbolizing witness, sacrifice, testing, courage and illumination.

ORIGINS

The name Unitarian refers historically to those who believed in the unity of God in distinction from those who believed in the trinity. The establishment of Unitarian attitudes often pre-dated the official use of the name which first occurred in Transylvania in the 1600's. Unitarianism in Canada finds its direct roots in the Non-subscribing Presbyterians of Ireland. However, close connections also exist with the Unitarian movement in England and Scotland, and with the development of Unitarianism in New England in the early 19th century.

Universalist congregations were active in Canada from the 1830's. Universalism began as a revolt against the harsh doctrine of salvation for a select few and, instead, proclaimed that all would be saved by a loving God. Some Canadians in our denomination call themselves Unitarian Universalists in proud acceptance of the dual heritage of the Canadian movement.

This Chapter has been provided by:
Ellen K. Campbell
Executive Director
Canadian Unitarian Council
188 Eglinton Avenue East, Suite 706
Toronto, Ontario
M4P 2X7
(416) 489-4121

[15] *Singing the Living Tradition*, Boston, Massachusetts: Beacon Press, 1993. ISBN 1-55896-260-3

THE WICCAN CHURCH OF CANADA

ORIGINS (FOUNDER)

By tradition, the words "Wiccan Church" constitute an oxymoron. Historically, Wiccans have met in small private groups called covens. These covens are thoroughly autonomous, although many identify themselves as belonging to "traditions" which share a commonality of practice and initiatory lineage. For the working chaplain, this can mean that a Wiccan client may find that the Wiccan Church of Canada representative is not an adequate care giver, and may request visitation from a member of his or her own coven. It is important to grant such a request, if the chaplain can do so.

The Wiccan Church of Canada (WCC) was incorporated in August 1979, a legal and public face for the traditionally private Wiccan worship.

NATURE OF RELIGION

Polytheistic

Wicca is a contemporary attempt to revive the spiritual tradition of pre-Christian Britain. As such, it is intimately associated with attempts to reconstruct the ancient worship practices of other pre-Christian civilizations, such as the Greek, Norse, Celtic, Sumerian or Egyptian. Forms of worship are both updated to meet twentieth century religious needs and back dated to encompass the on-going archaeological and anthropological study of ancient religious practices.

SCRIPTURES

The principal document from which a Wiccan conducts his or her worship is called a *Book of Shadows*. This is a collection of ritual scripts and other notes which the individual chooses to record. Every *Book of Shadows* is different. As rituals are added to the book, they provide a record of experience which will guide the individual Wiccan in the creation of more rituals. Other notes may include food recipes, commentaries about dreams, or records of oracles. An experienced Wiccan's *Book of Shadows* can provide the basic text and teaching by which traditions are handed down to further generations. Traditionally, the *Book of Shadows* is hand written, but the *Disk of Shadows* is becoming common in our computerized age.

In addition, classical works which record ancient religions before the coming of Christianity are often held as sources of sacred wisdom. These include: the *Eddas*, the *Mabinogion*, the *Egyptian Book of the Dead*, and the works of such classical writers as Hesiod, Lucretius, Homer, Sophocles, Cicero and Euripides.

BASIC BELIEFS

There have been, and continue to be, very many Gods and Goddesses. They are distinguished by the times and places in which they were worshipped, and by the natural forces or human endeavours over which they rule. Deities who rule over human works are held to be exemplars of excellence in their areas of expertise; human efforts in those areas are considered as offerings to those deities.

A Law of Nature exists, as implacable as that of gravity, which dictates that no action can occur without having significant repercussions throughout the world, eventually returning to affect the original actor. This Law is often referred to as Karma, and sometimes as the three fold law, suggesting that whatever one does will eventually affect him or her with three times the force of the initial action.

The principal deity to which we as earthly occupants need to address ourselves is the Earth Herself. She is often known as Mother Nature, and our industrial society appears to be killing Her. Virtually all Wiccans agree that their faith compels a vital concern for ecological issues.

MODE OF WORSHIP

The principal form of worship among Wiccans is usually called "ritual" or "circle". This is because the worshippers gather in a circle. Exact procedures vary, but the following steps, or ones similar, are usually observed:

The Ritual Bath: A time for meditation and focusing upon the ritual's intent, for clearly visualizing what one needs to pray for. It purifies the body prior to entering the sacred space of circle. The bath may employ aromatic herbs and oils.

Casting the Circle: A process of claiming the space in which the worship will occur, and making an area sacred for the duration of the ritual. We do this because for many centuries we did not have temples, and so we are accustomed to creating a sacred ground each time we gather for worship. This is often done by carrying a sword around the periphery of the worship space, but in Correctional settings the sword is usually replaced with a staff or wand.

Sweeping the Circle: This is accomplished with a broom, and begins the process of making the claimed space clean enough to invite the Gods to enter.

Elemental Purifications: This involves carrying symbols of the four elements of Air, Fire, Water and Earth around the circle to blow, burn, wash away or bury any unwanted spiritual presences.

Elemental Evocations: This involves calling to the spirits of each of the four elements to guard the circle, keeping it safe during the rite. Since we believe that absolutely everything is composed of these elements, each elemental spirit is therefore in charge of one quarter of all existence. Such potent spirits make good guardians of the circle. The spirit of Air lives to the east, and is asked to guard that direction. Similarly the spirit of Fire guards the south, Water the west, and Earth the north.

Calls to the God and/or Goddess are next. The Deity or Deities in charge of whatever is needful are asked to attend the circle. If healing is needed, healing gods or goddesses are called. If our prayer is to tell the stories of the Gods, then a bardic deity is called, and so on.

The Wine Blessing:	This celebrates the union of God and Goddess, and the creation of the Universe. The officiating priest dips the blade of a dagger (called an athame) into a cup of wine held by the officiating priestess. The sexual symbolism is obvious. The child of this union is Blessing, which is shared by all present as the wine is then consumed. In Correctional settings, a wand and unfermented grape juice or de-alcoholized wine are used, but the symbolism remains the same.
The Cake Blessing:	A short prayer thanking the gods for food and asking their blessing on the meal. The cakes are shared along with the wine. They represent the gods' bounty in providing the necessities of life. They are often crescent shaped, in honour of the lunar Goddess.
Libations:	These are made of the last of the wine and cakes, returning the gods' gifts from whence they came, that the gods too may take strength from them.
Energy Raising:	This may involve singing, dancing, theatrical performance or any other activity which honours the invited Deities. Wiccans believe that the results of prayer depend upon both the clarity with which one visualizes what one is praying for, and on the amount of effort which is put into that prayer.
	Thanksgiving and farewells to God, Goddess, and the elemental guardians are given to reflect the evocations and calls.
Closing the Circle	

STRUCTURE

Wiccan adherents may attend weekly worship services at local temples of the WCC in Toronto, Hamilton or Ottawa. During the summer, services are often held in local parks. Adherents may also attend public classes in the lore of the Gods, held on a weekly basis at the temples. A student who does well in these classes may apply to a priest or priestess for further tutorial training. A tutorial student may be recognized as a neophyte if his or her instructor feels that the student has a calling. The tutor may bring the neophyte before the assembled priesthood in a council meeting to determine whether he or she is ready for initiation into the priesthood. The examination process includes written, oral and practical ritual performance components.

DIVISIONS/DENOMINATIONS

Wicca is divided into "traditions", groups of covens bonded by a common initiatory lineage and common details in ritual practice. Two of the more prominent ones in Canada are:

Gardnerian/Alexandrian: The early forms of Wicca, formed when the last anti-witchcraft law was repealed in Britain in the early 1950s. [For further information call David Slater at (613)-230-0800.]

Covenant of Gaia: A matrifocal group of covens centred in Calgary, also operating in British Columbia. [For further information call: Bronwen Stonecypher at (403)-246-3456.]

RITUALS

Rituals are a large part of the Wiccan faith. Rituals are tied to the event with which they are performed, and so they are not reiterated here. For a detailed description of Wiccan ritual, please refer to the sections entitled *Mode of Worship* above, and *Holy Days/Festivals* below.

LAWS

Within the Wiccan World there are several codes of conduct which have become law. Generally they provide rules to settle disputes, instructions for maintaining the security and privacy of one's fellow Wiccans, procedures to create new covens, limits on the acceptable uses of money within the religious community, and instructions for caring and maintaining sacred objects. A copy of the code of laws commonly used by the WCC is available upon request.

The most often quoted guideline to Wiccan moral thought is the instruction usually called the Rede: "An it harm none, do what you will." While this statement does not quite hold the force of Law within the Wiccan community, it is universally held to be very good advice. It lays upon each Wiccan an obligation to think very carefully about the potential consequences of any action, before one acts.

MODE OF DRESS/MODESTY REQUIREMENTS

Wiccans often wish to wear a consecrated pendant in the form of a pentacle (interlaced five pointed star within a circle) as an expression of their faith and a constant reminder of their communion with the gods and a search for excellence. Many covens have a consecrated symbol which identifies members and provides spiritual connection. Such consecrated items must not be removed or handled by anyone but the wearer.

Some covens require that their members wear robes within the worship circle, and some worship skyclad (nude). Within the public worship circles offered by the WCC it is usually considered poor manners to wear very bright colours. Members are encouraged to wear robes, often girt with a braided cord belt. These are consecrated items and should be worn only during worship. Aside from this, there are no other dress requirements.

DIETARY REQUIREMENTS

Wiccans follow a variety of different Gods and Goddesses, some of whom strongly disapprove of various foods. A Wiccan whose personal worship is strongly focused on such a deity should therefore avoid eating the foods upon which that God or Goddess frowns. Thus, a Wiccan who is devoted to a God or Goddess who protects animals needs to maintain a vegetarian diet. There are however, no general prohibitions. Feast foods should be prepared by Wiccans, as preparation is a sacred act of offering to the Gods.

HOLY DAYS/FESTIVALS

Yule:

On the winter solstice, this is the celebration of the re-birth of the sun, as the short winter days begin to get longer. The Yule tree is dressed with fruit to remind the Gods of our need for a fruitful coming summer. Candles are lit to represent the sun.

Ritual foods include venison, goose, fruit breads and puddings, nuts, spiced wine or hot cider.

Solitary Observance may involve dressing a small tree with fruit or nuts, lighting yellow candles or incense, drinking a toast to the Sun, and pouring a libation to the passing of winter.

Imbolc:

Usually observed on February 2, this is a festival of light and fire. Corn dolls are burned as offerings to the sun, to speed His return. Remnants of this Pagan festival are found in Christian worship as the feast of St. Brigid.

Ritual foods include salted meats, breads, fruit preserves and red wine.

Solitary observance may involve lighting incense and a red candle, then using the candle to light a small corn doll or a few ears of grain in a cauldron or other fireproof container. Pour a libation on the ashes after drinking a toast to the Goddess who draws the Sun back to Her.

Ladyday:

On the spring equinox, this celebrates the spring. Spring is often envisioned as a Maiden Goddess who returns from the land of the dead where She spent the winter. One of Her names is Eostre, from which the word Easter is derived.

Ritual foods include fowl, seed breads, pancakes and white wine.

Solitary observance may involve lighting incense and green candles to welcome new growth, making a garland of flowers to wear through the day and pouring a libation in the garden.

Beltain: Celebrated on April 30, this is widely regarded as the mating day of the Sun God and Earth Goddess, whose marriage will provide the fruit of the harvest. Maypole dances today are hold-overs from Pagan fertility rites.

Ritual foods include eggs, rabbit and wine flavoured with woodruff.

Solitary observance may include painting eggs with growth and fertility symbols, meditations on a brown candle, and pouring libations in the wildest places that one can.

Litha: On the summer solstice, this is a celebration of the Sun at the height of His power.

Feast foods include berries, veal, new vegetables and Mead (honey wine).

Solitary observance may include lighting incense and white candles, rising before dawn to greet the sunrise, drinking a toast to the sun and pouring a libation in the garden.

Lammas: Usually observed on August 2, this is a celebration of the first harvest of grain. In Ontario this is usually corn. The Corn King is honoured even as He is cut down in the harvest.

Feast foods include corn bread, blueberries, beef, seafoods and beer.

Solitary observance may involve lighting incense and a blue candle to represent the summer sky. Make a doll from corn husks. Drink a toast to the Corn King, pour a small libation on the doll and put it away to be burned next Imbolc.

Harvestide: Celebrated on the fall equinox, this is another harvest festival. Apples are juiced for cider and grapes for wine. The communal effort of the harvest dictates the spiritual thoughts of the people.

Feast foods include apples, game birds, pears and ale.

Solitary observance may involve lighting incense and orange candles, and meditations on fruit and grain. Make a libation of the fruit and grain after your meditations by burying part of them in the garden.

Samhain: Celebrated on October 31, this is the feast of the dead. Animals which cannot be fed through the winter are slaughtered, bringing an awareness of mortality. The spirits of those who have died in the last year are invited to a final celebration.

Feast foods include pork, bread, root crops and red wine. All foods are cooked without salt. No salt should be used in the preparation or consumption of this feast.

Solitary observance may include lighting incense and black candles, then calling the name of someone who has died. Then put 3 pennies into a libation bowl and call the name again. Then lay a plate of food as an offering to the dead and call the name a third time. Eat your meal in silence, meditating and communing with the spirit person you have called. Place the food of the dead outside on the earth, just after sunrise.

BELIEFS AND PRACTICES REGARDING DEATH

BELIEFS

Contemporary:	Many gods and goddesses are spirits of excellence in all activities and ancient cultures.
Norse:	The life of the deceased determines the home of the God to which he or she will go.
Greco-Roman:	Several afterlife realms, some of which are resting places before reincarnation.
Egyptian:	The physical body lives again in an afterlife.
Celtic:	Life force is dispersed to realms of earth, sea and sky as the body decomposes.

PRACTICES

Contemporary:	Personal religious objects are usually cremated on an open pyre.
Norse:	Rites vary according to which home the deceased is thought to be going. Cremation with small offerings is common.
Greco-Roman:	Cremation or burial without embalming. External symbols of mourning such as black arm bands are worn until the mourner feels that his or her loss has healed.
Egyptian:	Extensive embalming is traditional, but is giving way today to environmental concern.
Celtic:	Burial without embalming assists the body's return to nature. Wakes (parties in honour of the deceased) release the departed's debts and obligations, so as to send his or her spirit off free of old bonds.

If a Wiccan dies while in institutional care, the chaplain or some other staff member should call the deceased's pastoral care giver. Where there is no record of such a person, the chaplain should call the WCC in case instructions have been given concerning the nature of the rites requested.

There are no restrictions on autopsy unless specified in writing in either the will or other instructions left by the deceased.

SPECIAL RELIGIOUS RITUALS (RITES OF PASSAGE) WHICH CAN BE PERFORMED ONLY BY AN AUTHORIZED REPRESENTATIVE OF THIS FAITH

Wiccaning:	The naming and blessing of children.
Dedication:	The rite of public declaration of one's commitment to the Gods.
Betrothal:	A formalization of engagement to be handfasted (married) after one year.
Handfasting:	A wedding. It is so called because the couple is ritually tied together at the wrist for the duration of the wedding celebration.
Handparting:	This involves severing the bonds formed at handfasting, with an equitable agreement on dispersal of common property and/or child custody and visitation.
First Blood:	The recognition of a young woman's coming of age, performed by the women of the community following the girl's first menstruation.
Rite of Manhood:	The recognition of a young man's coming of age, performed by the men of the community following the "breaking" of the voice or the appearance of facial hair.
Trimesters:	Blessings of pregnancy performed by the women of the community. The ceremony is led by a priestess who has born a child. These three rituals are performed during the three trimesters of pregnancy.
Passing the Veil:	A funeral. The rite varies according to the cultural bases of the departed's closest deities.
Neophyting:	Recognition that a student possesses a calling to the priesthood.
Initiation:	Admittance to the Wiccan priesthood.

SACRED WRITINGS REQUIRED

Wiccans in the care of governmental institutions need access to the books described above in the section entitled *Scriptures*.

They also require access to the large body of Wiccan literature which explains and illuminates the scriptural material, thereby helping the individual Wiccan incorporate it into his or her daily worship. Some examples are:

Adler, *Drawing Down the Moon.*
Starhawk, *The Spiral Dance.*
Cunningham, *Wicca, a Guide for the Solitary Practitioner.*
Gundarson, *Teutonic Religion.*

SACRED OBJECTS REQUIRED

Wiccans in the care of governmental institutions require access to an athame or wand, a chalice, wine or fruit juice, incense, candles, candle holders, charcoal, spring or rain water, salt, anointing oil, a living plant, God and/or Goddess images, herbs for ritual bathing, a dark coloured cotton robe, a libation bowl, tarot cards and other special occasion items brought by visiting priesthood.

In Correctional institutions, a wand should be used rather than the athame and fruit juice should be used instead of wine.

SYMBOLS

Wiccans use a variety of symbols in their worship.

SCHOOLS AND INSTITUTIONS

There are several mail-order schools of Wicca, or Witchcraft. They send lesson assignments and mark homework for correspondence students. Two such schools are the Church and School of Wicca in New Bern, North Carolina and Our Lady of Enchantments, in New Hampshire.

LUNAR CELEBRATIONS

Wiccans traditionally gather for worship when the moon is either new or full. The new moon is held to be an auspicious time to offer thanks for the successful completion of old projects, and prayers for help in new ones.

The full moon is held to be a time of great magical energy, a good time for putting a lot of effort into one's spiritual life and work. It helps to do this out of doors in the moonlight.

POSITION ON MILITARY SERVICE

Individuals who serve a peaceful deity may request a non-combat assignment, or may feel moved to conscientious objection. This is a personal decision and should be honoured as a sacred obligation, but such an obligation is not universal among Wiccans.

MEDICAL TREATMENT

Generally, there are no restrictions on medical treatment, but the patient must be permitted to contact his or her coven to request a healing rite. If the individual is not a coven member, he or she should contact the WCC for such a request. If the individual wishes a laying on of hands, this should be allowed. At the bedside, the use of talismans and shrines dedicated to healing deities is an important part of the healing process.

MEANS OF GAINING NEW MEMBERS

Wicca does not proselytize. New members find us through their own inquiries, through public lectures we are sometimes invited to present at schools and colleges, or as a result of media coverage.

RELATIONSHIP TO OTHER RELIGIONS

Wicca teaches its members to respect all gods, and to worship their own.

This chapter was written by HPS Tamarra James
For further information, please contact:

The Wiccan Church of Canada
1555 Eglinton Avenue West
Toronto, Ontario
M6E 2G9
(416) 781-2123

or:

HPS Tamarra James
9 Frank Crescent
Toronto, Ontario
M6G 3K6
(416) 656-7741

ZOROASTRIANISM

FOUNDER

Zoroaster (Zarathushtra) - Born in antiquity in Iran.

NATURE OF RELIGION

Monotheistic

SCRIPTURES

Khordeh Avesta: Selected prayers for daily use

Yasna: Principle text

Yashts:	Hymns
Visparad:	Invocations
Vandidad:	Religious laws

BASIC BELIEFS

The belief in one Supreme Creator - Ahura Mazda (The Omnipotent, Omniscient and Omnipresent Lord).

Life is a struggle between good and evil.

The importance of following the path of Asha (Righteousness), based on three fundamental guiding principles of Good Thoughts, Good Words and Good Deeds.

The ultimate triumph of Good over Evil, leading to Perfection and Immortality at the Renovation.

Belief in Fire as representing the Glorious Radiant Spirit of God.

MODE OF WORSHIP

Worship is primarily individual.

Community worship and rituals take place on holy days.

Houses of worship are known as fire temples.

STRUCTURE

Priests are ordained from traditionally hereditary families of priests.

High priests are associated with major fire temples.

DIVISIONS/DENOMINATIONS

Zoroastrianism has three divisions, primarily based on observance of different calendars:

Shenshahi

Kadimi

Fasli

RITUALS

Navjote:	Initiation into the faith.
Marriage:	Performed by the duly ordained priests.
Death:	Primary funerary services and practices performed for four days by priests.

Padyab-Kusti:	Involves washing exposed bodily parts, and the untying and retying of the sacred thread (Kusti) several times a day.
Jashan:	The most common communal celebration.
Ceremonies for the departed:	Performed during the year following death and thereafter, on each death anniversary.

LAWS

Celibacy is not advocated even amongst priests.

Members are enjoined to preserve and protect all of nature's creations in the environment.

MODE OF DRESS/MODESTY REQUIREMENTS

A white undershirt called the Sudreh and a woolen cord called the Kusti, worn around the waist after initiation.

No specific dress codes, but common sense and modesty are expected at all times.

The head is traditionally covered at prayer times and in fire temples.

DIETARY REQUIREMENTS

No dietary restrictions on food or drink, except moderation.

HOLY DAYS/FESTIVALS

Naoroz:	New Year's Day.
Khordadsal:	Birthday of Prophet Zoroaster.
Fraverdegan (Muktad):	Remembrance days for the departed.
Gahambars:	Six seasonal festivals commemorating each stage of creation.
Death Anniversary of Zoroaster	

BELIEFS AND PRACTICES REGARDING DEATH

BELIEFS

Belief in the immortality of the soul. Belief in the concept of divine judgement and the state of the soul in Heaven or Hell depending on the choice made between the good and the evil in life.

PRACTICES

Preparation of the body consisting of ritual bath and wearing of the sacred symbols of the sudreh and kusti.

Four day funerary practices performed by priests.

Presently, cremation or burial in North America.

SPECIAL RELIGIOUS RITUALS WHICH CAN BE PERFORMED ONLY BY AN AUTHORIZED REPRESENTATIVE OF THIS FAITH

Navjote:	Initiation into the faith.
Wedding:	Religious service and blessings to the wedded couple.
Jashan:	The most common communal celebration. Thanksgiving or remembrance of the departed.
Navar/Maratab:	Ordination of a priest.
Nahan:	A ritual purification bath.

Higher liturgical ceremonies such as Yasna and ceremonies for the departed.

SACRED WRITINGS REQUIRED

Religious observance does not require the presence of any sacred writings.

SACRED OBJECTS REQUIRED

Fire, Divo (oil lamp), etc.

SYMBOLS

Fire:	It is regarded as the manifestation of the Divine Spirit.
Fravashi:	Depicted as a winged figure. It is the Divine Essence in every single object of creation including man. A guardian angel.
Sudreh:	A white undershirt worn after initiation. Carries a symbolic bag near the heart to gather good deeds.
Kusti:	A woolen cord worn around the waist after initiation.

This chapter was written by:
Religious Committee
Zoroastrian Society of Ontario
3590 Bayview Avenue
Willowdale, Ontario   M2M 3S6
(416) 733-4586

Appendix A

OTHER TRADITIONS

The Ontario Multifaith Council on Spiritual and Religious Care put forth a significant effort to include as many diverse faith traditions as possible.

For various reasons, many organizations contacted either chose not to participate in this reference manual, or simply did not return the required information to the Multifaith Council. Such groups include the following:

The Antiochian Orthodox Christian Church
The Apostolic Church in Canada
The Associated Gospel Churches
The Byelorussian Autocephalic Orthodox Church
The Church of the Nazarene
The Church of United Brethren in Christ
The Churches of Christ
The Evangelical Baptist Church
The Evangelical Fellowship of Canada
The Greek Orthodox Church
The Lutheran Church of Canada
The Mennonite Brethren Church
The Missionary Church of Canada
The New Apostolic Church
The New Dawn Moravian Church
The Romanian Orthodox Church
The Russian Orthodox Church
The Serbian Orthodox Church
The Spiritualist Church
The Ukrainian Catholic Church
The Ukrainian Greek Orthodox Church
The Weslayan Church of Canada

Many of these groups expressed an interest to participate in the next edition of the Multifaith Information Manual. We will welcome their participation.

Appendix B

Ontario Multifaith Council on Spiritual and Religious Care
Publishing Trust Committee

The Publishing Trust Committee of the OMCSRC develops and makes available multifaith resource materials to assist Chaplains and spiritual care-givers. A totally self-sustaining service, any revenue over costs is directed to the further development and subsidy of new resources. The following are some of the items currently available. Write us to be placed on our mailing list.

Multifaith Clipart Book $15.95

Set of 11 Faith Symbol Banners $659.00

"Rainbow" Multifaith Banner $199.95

Write for information about individual 'stick-on' multifaith symbols. These will be priced below $30.00 each. They will adhere to almost any surface to enhance a worship centre.

Clipart can be made available in most digital formats. Write to request prices, specifying your equipment, applications, and preferred disk type and file format.

Ontario Multifaith Council on Spiritual and Religious Care
Publishing Trust Committee
35 McCaul St., Suite 200
Toronto, ON M5T 1V7
CANADA

Phone: (416) 326-6858
FAX: (416) 326-6867